The Many Faces of Women

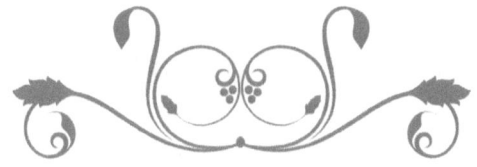

TERESA RENDA CARLSON

FOREWORD BY LICIA CARLSON

3 SWALLYS PRESS
BOSTON

Copyright © 2021 by Teresa Renda Carlson
Cover design by Pam Germer
All rights reserved

Paperback ISBN 978-0-9987651-6-7
1. Personal Memoirs. 2. Biography & Autobiography—Women

To my Licia and all the other women in my world

Let us be grateful to people who make us happy; they are the charming gardeners who make our souls blossom.
Thank you.

—Marcel Proust

CONTENTS

Caryatids: A Foreword by Licia Carlson	vii
Acknowledgments	xi
Introduction	1
1. Images of Capistrano Women	8
2. International Faces	20
3. Michigan Faces	36
4. The Women in My Family	67
5. My Immediate Family	77
6. The Ladies, My Special Teachers	110
7. Two Faces from Boston	127
8. My Mother	135
9. Reflections from My Diary	162
10. Reunited	206
Post Scriptum	215

Caryatids: A Foreword

This book is deeply personal for me, but it also speaks to many universal themes: love, loss, friendship, hardship, and the depth of bonds that we can create between ourselves and others. My mother was blessed with four sisters, each incredible in her own way. But all of the women in this book constitute a sisterhood, one that has provided love, wisdom, comfort, care, nourishment, laughter and joy. They are women who represent a range of cultures, ages, professions, passions, talents, and they have each given unique gifts to their families, friends and communities. To bring them together in this book shows how the threads of their lives have been intertwined and have brought color and texture to the fabric of my mother's life, and to mine as well.

As I read the portraits of these amazing women, the image of the caryatid came to mind. Caryatids were statues that adorned many ancient buildings and temples. Though occupying a similar stance and often dressed alike, each was individually designed and had her own unique features. Standing side by side, regal and beautiful, they appear to be holding up these massive structures. This is how I imagine the women in this book: solidly, proudly, eternally bearing and sustaining the weight of their individual and collective worlds. Each one is necessary and indispensable; together, they are even more powerful.

Four caryatids at the Erechtheum, Acropolis, Athens, Greece

Since antiquity, artists have continued to represent caryatids in various ways. One of our favorite twentieth-century artists, the Italian Amedeo Modigliani, made over seventy drawings of caryatids intended to be preliminary sketches for a "temple to humanity" that would be held up by them. Though he only completed one statue, the fleshy, nude images of these caryatids crouched, curved, and in some cases bowing under the weight they are holding, are a departure from the straight, elegant, fully draped Greek caryatids. Yet both images represent aspects of women's lives. Modigliani referred to them as "columns of tenderness," a phrase that echoes in my mind as I read about the love and care that the women in this book have given.[1]

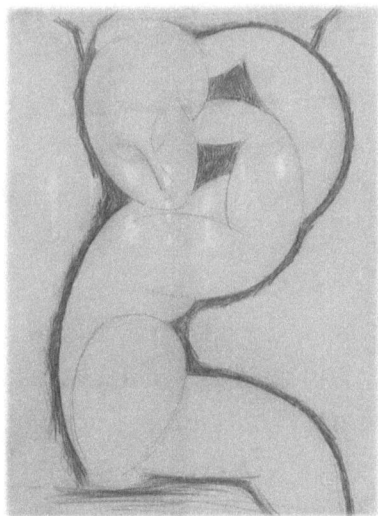

Caryatids, by Amedeo Modigliani

---

[1] https://www.tate.org.uk/art/artworks/modigliani-caryatid-t00149

THE MANY FACES OF WOMEN

Feminist philosophers have spoken a lot about the importance of care, dependency, and our fundamental *inter*dependence as members of the human community. In the past, these were relegated to the "feminine" realm: dependency was considered a sign of weakness, and care represented "woman's work." And yet these stories show that care has many faces and requires tremendous strength. Caregiving is a reciprocal act of love between giver and recipient. And all of us at times are dependent, and are mutually *interdependent* upon each other for our joys and in our sorrows.

From what I can gather, most artists who created caryatids were men, likely crafting them as they saw women. The portraits of caryatids in this book, however, have been painted by Teresa's insightful and careful hand. And while they represent tenderness and beauty, they are also columns of strength, fortitude and resolve. With her wisdom and artistry, she offers a glimpse of the many women who have graced her remarkable life's temple.

This book can be read as a letter of thanks, a gift of love, and a celebration of women's lives. For me, I read it as a daughter filled with admiration, deep gratitude, and profound love for the woman who holds us up every day.

Licia Carlson
September 2021

Acknowledgments

I would like to thank Licia, my daughter, who led me through my pilgrimage since she was eight months old, and continued to the present, reading my manuscripts and contributing to them;

My husband Thomas, who read each manuscript and patiently and tirelessly edited them;

My readers, who encouraged me to continue, anxious for the next book;

And Nivi, my editor in chief, who brought my words to light in a wonderful, creative, artistic way.

Introduction

I spent the first seventeen years of my life mostly with women, old and young, in a mountainous little village in the Apennines, which, although insignificant in the world at large, a little grain of sand on the beaches of life, a microcosm of the greater universe, had great influence on me and formed me physically and spiritually. Capistrano was a little village that beamed with life and primordial forces strong enough to shake the earth that gave it hospitality.

The women were the strength of the village, remarkable in their ability to endure adversities of every size and shape. They were the givers of life, the mothers to all, nourishing the young, the old, and the sick and the sufferers; no one died alone, even in the pandemic of 1918, when everyone, armed with a handkerchief and vinegar as disinfectant, visited those dying of it. The able ones went to live in the country with their families to avoid contact with others; not unlike the tales of Boccaccio, an Italian writer who describes in his opus *The Decameron* the exodus out of Florence to the country by citizens who feared the plague in the Middle Ages.

Similar, too, were the women of the 1930s and the 1940s, valiant warriors who braved famine, bombs and destruction, who saw their husbands dragged out of their houses, some shot, some beaten and thrown into rivers after being forced to swallow bottles of castor oil and left to die for refusing to wear the black shirts as ordered by Mussolini, who created a reign of terror in the late thirties; women who were left to collect these wounded men, the women who would pull them out of the rivers like beaten fish by the light of an olive lamp, only to repeat the process again and again. My mother was one of those brave women. I met many remarkable women in this little village, some who left deep impressions on me, others whose generosity kept me alive by breastfeeding me as an infant, others who loved me so deeply that they taught me how to love in return, others, like Peppina, who protected me from the ridicule and bullying of other children. To all of them I dedicate this book and my devotion until my last breath.

INTRODUCTION

An Ode to Joyful Ladies
By Aala Zahra Mosallaei

Every woman
Starts as a baby,
Lying in her crib,
Staring at anyone who passes by
With big eyes
Filled with enough love for everybody
In the universe.
When you visit the bakery in town
The baker smiles at the baby's adorable eyes filled with
love.
When she laughs
That small baby girl
Who is less than three feet tall
Puts a smile on even the grumpiest of faces.
She spreads joy in the small house,
And nobody is seen angry in her presence,
For a baby girl is filled with love and joy.

Then as the baby turns into a toddler
She can also be named a sister,
Toddling around the house
And playing with her little sibling,
Sometimes helping mama in the kitchen
When she makes cookies for her uncle
Who comes over on the weekends.
Her funny frolics
Make the whole family laugh.

She comes home from preschool
Singing a song,
Making the night joyful with her words.

And now the toddler is no longer,
But she is a girl
Hurrying to help her mother with the chores after
school,
Helping her little sibling
Who is trying to learn the ABC's,
Painting pictures for her father's wall,
Writing shopping lists
And telling stories of school
At night.
When she is taken to the grocery store
She helps find what they need
And helps in every way she can.
All day
And all night.

The girl, now a woman,
Goes to college to study,
Hoping one day,
If she has a family,
To become a doctor
To support her family,
Studying hard
All day
And still bringing her usual joy around with her.

INTRODUCTION

The mother now
Plays with her children
And makes delicious dinners,
Spending the day
In the kitchen,
Preparing food.
And when she's not,
She works
So that she can put her child
In a good school
When the child grows up.
She makes everyone laugh
And tells the best
Bedtime stories
That will make any child fall asleep.
She teaches a great many things
And helps with homework
And plays
With her child,
Putting the joy she has
In her child.

And now
Her grandchildren
And great-grandchildren
Hug her.
She is still spreading joy
To everybody:
The neighborhood children
Who turn to her for advice,

The baker,
Whom she buys a cinnamon roll from every day,
Her children,
Grandchildren,
And great-grandchildren.
And for as long as she lives
She will keep spreading joy.

My Aala is the ten-year-old who lives next door to us with her parents, Afsaneh and Hossein, and her older brother Ali. She is brought up by two loving parents who dedicate lots of time to their children, despite their demanding professions.

Back: Ali, Tom, Julian. Front: Aala, Afsaneh, Teresa

INTRODUCTION

I learned and continue to learn many lessons about living from them. Afsaneh, with her open smile, radiates love and holiness, understanding and forgiveness; good lessons for me, given my volcanic Italian character. Aala taught me to listen and appreciate my gardening, for she is an avid lover of plants from my Mother Earth. I spend time with Aala, Ali and Afsaneh in my kitchen making biscotti, cornetti and pizzas, which both our families love.

Writing this book on the women who influenced me in life, I asked Aala if she would write something for the book, and she came up with the poem above. She and I are also writing a children's book on an ancient Iranian fable, which Aala is also illustrating. We temporarily halted the project because of the 2020 Covid pandemic, with the hope we will soon continue writing in my garden, which we both love.

1

Images of Capistrano Women

I was surrounded by women in my little village; it seemed that there were more women than men, many of whom had emigrated to other lands: Canada, Australia, South America, in search of better lives. The women stayed behind taking care of the family and the land, working like mules from dawn to sunset, leaving the children to the old ladies to keep an eye on them, or to nature to be nurtured by its vast gifts: wild fruits, flowers, rivers and hills to climb, a little paradise for all of us to explore and enjoy. It was an idyllic life for the children, a life free from any constraints, free like the wind to blow anywhere their imagination led them. Among this paradise were also old people who suffered unbearable diseases alone, no family left to take care of them, relying solely on the kindness of the women of the village for their survival. My mother took care of many of them, teaching us children also to care for them, saying no one is too young to help. What teaching moments. I always did cherish and admire women, and here are some of the faces of the women of the village, an integral part of the mosaic that is me.

ANNEIA

A tall, slim woman who lived most of her life supine. At least that's how I saw her during my seventeen years of living in Capistrano. My mother organized some of the women to help Anneia with daily needs. In the morning she was brought out of her dark, lugubrious, windowless abode on her bed, where she lay all day until the same ladies took her in after sunset. My mother was in charge of the worst job, washing her and then taking her soiled clothes to the river to be washed. Then she would bring them back home and set them in a clay container with a protruding hole and pour scalding water with cinders, used as disinfectant and whitening agent, over them. Then, back to the river to be rinsed and stretched over the ginestra bushes to dry under the bright, warm sun. Anneia was kept clean and smelling nicely with sprigs of lavender placed under her sheets.

We children kept her company, singing songs and scratching her feet to see her laugh, which showed her cavernous, toothless mouth. We danced the tarantella and other folk dances that she probably danced when she was young and erect, moving her tall, flexible, elegant limbs to the sound of flutes and harmonicas. We never saw her cry or get angry or complain. Hers was a life of acceptance, prayer and thankfulness. At the festivities, she participated by lying down at the entrance to the church, and everyone who entered bowed to her with reverence. She was part of all of us, united by proximity and by the example her valiant spirit set for us all. I loved gathering bouquets of wildflowers to bring to Anneia, whose wide smile would render me kinder and gentler, a great example of love and acceptance of suffering with joy, which later in my adult life came in useful, during my own arduous *cammin*. When she died we all mourned and missed her terribly.

PEPPINA

Another giant in my life was Peppina, a young woman who was mentally disabled, with a Herculean strength and ability to be everywhere in the village, especially when needed to separate warring children from each other. She was a gift to me and my sisters, defending us against any attack or taunting by the other children in the village; it felt like we had a private bodyguard. When children teased me for my odd looks, she would throw them on the ground and beat them until they asked me for pardon. Her devotion to us was due in part to my father having rescued her from a hospital for the mentally ill where, according to former residents, many patients were maltreated.

Apparently, my father went to visit Peppina there and found the conditions suspect, so he took Peppina by the arm and brought her home, over strong objections from the authorities. Peppina thrived in the freedom the village gave her, going from one street to the other, telling whomever she saw her version of coming home: "Mastro Fineo disse al direttore di Cilifarco, che brutto nome, Peppina non puo' stare qui', me la porto a casa." (Master Fineo said to the director of Cilifarco—what an ugly name—Peppina cannot stay here, I will bring her home.)

Peppina was loved by everyone in the village, treated with respect and kindness, and participated in every festivity of the village. She in turn helped the old ladies by going to the fountain to fill their jars with fresh water, helping mothers with their children, bringing food to the infirm, helping with unhusking corn, shelling beans and gathering olives together with us. We loved having her around. This acceptance of disability was reflected more recently to a family with two disabled children who returned from Canada to live in a more accepting environment in Capistrano. Peppina is still living as of the writing of this book. Unfortunately, she spends her time in a wheelchair, but poses for her brother, who is a painter and takes care of her. What a joy she has been for us all, stirring in our hearts love and kind acts toward others. She made us better people; thank God for our Peppina.

Painting of Peppina by her brother

DONNA MARIA

Donna Maria was a woman always dressed in black who lived alone in a tiny house with a bed, a little table with two wooden chairs, and a small chimney with a few pots, where she cooked her meals. Almost every night my mother would send her a hot dish of pasta, minestra or whatever she prepared for us. I always volunteered to take the food to her, for I was intrigued by this mysterious woman who stood erect and statuesque as she opened the door to let me in. She was noble in countenance, simple in her gestures, and warm in her acceptance of the food I brought, gently tapping my head with her venous, sinewy, long hands. I grew very attached to this colossal woman and often sat beside her in church with the irresistible urge to caress her hand. She would give me a reserved smile like a Madonna, of which there were many in our church. The one I loved most was the statue of the Madonna of the Rosary, refined and genteel like a noblewoman.

Donna Maria remained my great fascination. I sensed that to achieve such serenity she must have suffered a great deal, and I inquired about her life first of my mother and then of my father, who admired her strength and courage. No answer came from my parents. I resolved to ask my grandmother Dirce, and she explained in the simplest terms that Donna Maria had suffered a great deal braving a rather involved surgery without anesthesia, which was not available in the forties in my village. My mother was proud of her Fineo, my father, who assisted the doctor in preparation for the surgery by giving Donna Maria grappa to drink to numb her. In 1971, when I had my first mastectomy, my mother revealed that Donna Maria had undergone two mastectomies without anesthesia. What horror I felt in my being, what admiration I felt for this brave, strong and trusting woman to go through with the surgeries. I began to trust my instincts that this was an unusual woman whom I respected and loved.

Donna Maria

ANNINA

When I visited the Church of San Marco in Venice, some years later with my husband and daughter, admiring the beautiful mosaics, I was fascinated by what constituted a mosaic. Each mosaic, representing a religious figure, was made by assembling many small tiles, each different in color, but together forming a figure. I was so impressed that their images remained in my consciousness for many years. On the train back to Bologna I imagined myself as a mosaic made up of many women, each a tile forming the figure of a child, me, who one can say was brought up by the whole village.

Many were the women who put me to their breast as an infant famished during the Second World War, born during a bombing raid, causing my mother to lose her milk. My sister Nina would take me in her strong arms to the various women who had a newborn and begged them to give me a little of their milk; some she bribed with olive oil; others could not be bribed, for due to the famine, they were not producing much milk, barely enough for their own child.

Among these women was one, Annina, who welcomed me with open arms and let me nurse until I was full. What a generous woman, the wife of Michele, my father's best friend, whose advice to go to Rome with him and together help rebuild after the war, my father did not follow. Annina was for me the symbol of life, a river of beauty, generosity and love. I wanted to grow up and be like her, a kind and loving mother. She was for me a font of inspiration to bring to others the best that was in me.

Two summers ago in church in Capistrano, I kept admiring this beautiful woman sitting in the pew in front of me. I trembled with excitement when I saw her face, the face of Annina, the beautiful Annina who held me in her arms and fed me like her own child. I met my "milk" sister and spent many days talking with and blessing my Annina. To give is an act of generosity, but to give of one's self is an act of love.

RINUCCIA

Rinuccia was one of the most loved and admired women in Capistrano, for her friendliness, openness and her beautiful smile, which radiated warmth and love. She is the younger daughter of my mother's best friend, and I, a few years younger, admired her, although my sisters were closer to her. But things changed when she emigrated to Toronto, with her husband, Micuccio, an excellent tailor trained in Milan. A few years later, I ended up living in Toronto, not too far from Rinuccia. She loved my mother and visited us frequently, and we did the same, for she lived in Little Italy, where Micuccio had a tailor shop, and we passed by whenever we went shopping. She was always welcoming and would invite us for coffee with her and her delightful little girl, Maria. When I began teaching at Saint Francis of Assisi Elementary School, also in Little Italy, I would stop after school and have coffee, talk about her beloved Capistrano, which we both missed, and shed a few nostalgic tears together until Maria woke up from her afternoon nap and played the little piano I had given her, with such seriousness and delight that we both ended up remarking how talented she was.

After a few years, Rinuccia and her family moved away from Little Italy to a neighborhood north of Toronto on Yonge Street, a move which caused me great grief and took away from College Street, Little Italy, the joy that Rinuccia's presence brought me. I soon realized that it is not the place that is the most significant factor in our lives, but the people we cherish. I avoided going by Rinuccia's house after she left, recalling only the wonderful memories, like our talks of our beloved village, images of youth, hope and aspiration. We kept in touch, visiting each other, yet we did not have our spontaneous meetings, only planned ones, lacking spontaneity. We come from a village where everything evolved in a moment; no plans, no missing pre-arranged dates, seizing every moment as it presented itself. People dropped in at suppertime to the discomfort of no one; a chair and a plate were added with no sighs; sharing the little we had was our modus vivendi. We shared grief and joy, births and deaths, a life of the moment, with bells announcing it in the morning, at noon or in the evening, calling the villagers working in the fields to come home to a warm meal, to love or discord; a life lived consciously aware of the passing of time and the events that time discloses. Rinuccia and I shared a heritage where tears and laughter intersected, and then united to become one, just like the sweet waters of the river mix with the salty water of our seas to become one.

Teresa, Maria and Rinuccia

Rinuccia and I met in Capistrano over many summers when we returned to the village to visit our relatives and enjoy the brilliant sun that illuminated our shores, our hearts. We both became so euphoric that we would kiss and embrace everyone we met, an embrace of joy to be among those faces strong and malleable, faces aged and wrinkled by the strong rays of the sun, which greeted us in the morning and gave us the most beautiful sunsets, only to envelop later in the darkness of the night, lit by oil lamps hanging from every limb available. A hard but idyllic life full of mystery and awe.

IMAGES OF CAPISTRANO WOMEN

Rinuccia, Licia and Maria, Toronto, 2003

2

International Faces

CECILIA

Two black eyes with a piercing gaze looked at me as I was talking to my sister Gina, who was in the hospital for an autoimmune disease that was ravaging her brain. I looked back into those eyes, deep in their sockets; eyes that had seen a lot, that had known fear and hardships; eyes that also held a glint of joy. I went near her, lying in the bed next to my sister, took a closer look at her and she smiled at me. Like the Little Prince, who slowly and gently tried to befriend the fox, I went closer and asked if she needed some fresh water. A faint voice came from her skeletal body; she was on the last leg of her journey. I fetched the water, poured some into a plastic cup and brought it toward her mouth. She drank it quickly; she was thirsty. I sat beside her, held her hand and asked her name. I learned she was Italian, from Monte Cassino. I asked if she felt like telling me about her childhood, and after a long pause she drew in a long breath and began.

"I lived during the Second World War, and from January to May of 1944, I became part of the Italian Resistance; a girl of fifteen did not raise suspicion, so I was of great help bringing communications to the Allied Forces, who were fighting a series of battles to dislodge the German line installed on the mountain near Monte Cassino. The Germans did not destroy the ancient monastery, founded in the 1200s by Benedict of Norcia, because it contained many sacred manuscripts, which the Germans brought to the pope in Rome. The Allied Forces, however, bombed the monastery, thinking the Germans were orchestrating their attacks from there. The Germans were defeated in the battle of Monte Cassino, and on the way down, those remaining captured every human being during the retreat. I was holding a little boy crying in my arms who was separated from his parents. The soldiers in the military truck saw us and picked us up, throwing us in the back of the vehicle, together with others who had been captured. They told us to get off the truck in a secluded area and that we were going to be shot as traitors. My whole body shook but I was able to hold the little boy in my arms, who out of terror became unable to cry. As the German soldiers were ready to shoot, an English plane bombed them and the truck. We were miraculously spared. With my little boy in my arms I ran to a nearby wheat field and hid for almost a year, until the farmers came and told us the war was over. My little boy grew into a man, nurtured by my remaining family, most of whom were killed by the Germans, and as an eighteen-year-old emigrated to Canada. He kept sending me money, and a few years later he applied for me to join him in Toronto."

She told me that she felt much better now that she had emptied her soul of those horrid memories, and as she finished her sentence, who came into the room with a bouquet of flowers but her little boy, now a man. As Shakespeare says: "All's well that ends well." Her joy for life was palpable as she looked at that colossal man enter the room. I felt her happiness and suffered less knowing that she had somebody to visit her, even though she was confined to a bed in a room she shared with many others. Her world was limited, reduced to the minimum, yet her eyes shone like two stars that had left the heavens to be in her. I could not forget that story or its teller, contemplating a humanity that has millions of stories to tell. Each story is a gift to mankind, and especially to me, who spent an entire childhood listening to stories, some real, some mythical, and some life changing, like this last one. A story is the greatest gift I can receive.

JANINE

I knew her only as Janine; a beautiful, elegant lady with an air of nobility, displayed humbly and naturally, but furtively. She lived in a palace on Champs-Élysées in Paris, where the wealthy and noble lived, she being married to one of them. She lived a fairy tale story, happily married with two children. But the Second World War knocked at her door and she, being very patriotic, could not resist the call. She became part of the Resistance, a guerrilla-type of organization intent on liberating France from the invading Germans who occupied the city and formed the Vichy government. Janine was assigned to bring communications between the Resistance and the American headquarters, also in Paris. It was a dangerous mission for a lady used to the comforts of life, but she embraced it wholeheartedly, even though it meant the abandonment by her husband and children.

Unfortunately, after many successful missions she was captured by the Germans, and together with many others, she was brought to the central square to be shot as an example of German severity and a warning to others. As the captured were unloaded onto the square and ready to be rifled down, an airplane miraculously flew overhead and began to bomb the German soldiers, who, terrified, fled, leaving the prisoners free to be rescued. Janine found refuge at the American headquarters, and when the war ended she married an American soldier and moved to the U.S., ending up in Louisiana, where she had two daughters. On her way home from the hospital with her husband and her second baby, her husband had to make a sudden stop and Janine hit the dashboard, injuring her eyes. After many unsuccessful surgeries she lost her eyesight completely.

I met Janine in a suburb of Detroit through a dear friend, Mary Kelly, who, together with her husband Clyde, became a constant visitor, taking her out to eat or bringing warm dishes. I took to Janine right away and we too became friends. I helped her with meal preparation, and she especially liked the quiches I loved to make for her. The first time she came to my house for dinner, she noticed the French decor by feeling the chairs covered with velvet. She became happy to be there with all of us, including Marie (as she called Mary) and Clyde. I never forget the days that Janine blessed our house with her presence, infusing the rooms with a positive energy. She always smiled, never complained about her situation, and savored every moment of life. She told me her story in the most elegant French, with her musical Parisian accent, and special words that only Parisians have in their lexicon. We took many pictures to celebrate those days.

I cherished our weekly visits, speaking French and listening to her stories, which were elegantly told. I shared with her our immigrant roots and the difficulty of leaving one's country for another with totally different customs and traditions, a different style of living. To adapt is in a way to say goodbye to your ways and replace them with new ones, like different times for eating the main meals, different breakfasts, different ways of eating, like eating snacks all day. These seem like insignificant differences, but they are essential to the way we experience life both in America and in the old countries, where the main meal was eaten at noon, together, at the table, with a tablecloth, and not in front of a TV. Everyone would converse and celebrate the coming together, and each course seemed to bring a new topic of discussion. We missed the casualness, meeting people on the *passeggiata* (the evening walk), enjoying time together at a cafe without having made elaborate plans. The trip to the supermarket was a daily occurrence; everything was eaten fresh.

Mary Kelly, Janine and Teresa celebrating Janine's birthday at Teresa's house

How much I learned from Janine and her courage to live alone. Her second husband had died from Agent Orange, a defoliant that kills all vegetation and people who breathe it, including the soldiers in Vietnam. Janine could not use the stove to warm food, so she was grateful when we brought some warm soup. Her house was impeccably clean, by her bending down to the floor and picking up every speck of dirt she felt with her hands. She developed a strong sensation in her hands, and by feeling someone's face, she could describe them to perfection. Her hands became her eyes through which she could see the world.

She often wore soft pink cashmere sweaters which she washed by hand; she always looked perfect, her hair in place and beautiful. She was an inspiration to anyone who met and knew her. She spoke often about her involvement with the Resistance during the Second World War, her capture by the Germans, her escape from execution in the square and her ardent prayers to Saint Odile, her protectress, to save her and the others. "Teresa, I always carried a silver medal of Saint Odile in my pocket, and at that terrible moment as I stood in the square, head held high, my body trembling like a windswept tree, looking out to the crowd and saying goodbye to the world of the living, I felt the medal in my pocket and prayed that I would be brave. A calm descended on me and, like a cloud, enveloped me in her mist. I heard a rumbling above; a plane began bombing the German soldiers and we were saved." She gave me a medal of Saint Odile, to whom I pray in times of need.

Each meeting with Janine was a spiritual journey for me. Although we talked about external things like the war, I burrowed inwardly, learning more about myself and what was important. I was a gleaner, a listener, and blessed every moment I spent with my Janine.

URSULA

I was sitting on a bench waiting for my daughter's ballet lesson to finish, in a small but graceful park adorned by a statue of a couple embracing, in the center of Birmingham, Michigan, when a beautiful woman appeared, and seeing me reading a French book, she greeted me in French. She introduced herself as Ursula Strebel from Switzerland, residing in Birmingham with her husband, a pediatrician, and their three daughters, Catherine, Barbara and Theresa. I was struck by the presence of this woman, regal in appearance, intelligent in her comments and a linguist. She told me (in French) that she also spoke German and Swiss German fluently. Her French was impeccable, her German that of a native, and her English grammatically correct, as behooves those who speak several languages (with a delightful accent). We embarked on an engaging conversation that made us neglectful of the time, which did not particularly please my eight-year-old Licia, who greeted me with a piercing gaze after her long wait at the ballet school for me to pick her up.

Licia and I visited Ursula and her family soon after, and we liked the beautiful girls, full of life and energy. The youngest, Theresa, became our babysitter when my husband Thomas and I went out in the evening. Licia enjoyed her joyful laughter and would encourage us to go out so she could be with her Theresa. Ursula often invited us to partake of her wonderful crusty bread, right out of the oven and emanating a delightful aroma, a European bread, which, with butter and cheeses, delighted our taste buds. How I looked forward to those occasions when we were all sitting at her big wooden table, talking, laughing and eating. I had no idea how much I missed the European ways, where bread and cheese could become a feast, a celebration of the moment. Licia and Theresa would play the violin for us and then go into the garden to play while Ursula, Catherine, Barbara and I talked about our acculturation and the great differences between the two continents. I fell in love with this marvelous, intelligent family and I could not get enough of them. I met the two elder girls' boyfriends, delightfully intelligent and handsome men with whom I developed a friendship that allowed me to have marvelous discussions about their studies and aspirations for the future. What a treasure I found in Ursula and her family.

We met each other's husbands and had many evenings

together. Leon was a charming Alsatian and loved good food, skiing and mountain climbing with the whole family. But unfortunately, Leon soon left for Basel, Switzerland, to work as a researcher for a big drug company. He was tired of Children's Hospital in Detroit, where he worked as a pediatrician. Ursula was a nurse but was pursuing a nursing degree at Wayne State University. I admired her strength and ability to study physics, chemistry and math, difficult subjects for someone who had been out of school for quite a while; but despite the difficulty she carried on, determined to finish. I met her mother, who came to Detroit for her graduation. What an accomplishment! We were all very proud of her. Soon thereafter she got a job in a psychiatric hospital and worked a late afternoon shift that ended around two a.m. It was then that the fun began.

Every night at two, a little red car stopped outside my house, and quietly, like a mouse, Ursula would come in from the cold, after an exhausting trip down ominous Eight Mile Road, and collapse into a comfortable chair in front of a roaring fire which I kept going for her. My husband was deeply asleep and nothing would wake him up, so we had the house to ourselves, eating salami, her favorite, wonderful bread from her oven and drinking plenty of wine. She began talking about her Leon and how she missed him, yet not forgiving him for leaving her with the girls; eating, crying and sipping wine, I listening, she crying. After she had had enough time to vent her frustration, I would come up with some of my mother's sayings about men and we both would burst out laughing; tears and laughter, what a wonderful catharsis.

Another night Ursula came with a letter from Leon that was not particularly consoling, and again tears welled up in her beautiful eyes like water from a fountain. They seemed endless, until we had the idea to burn the letter. We watched it as it went up in flames, with a toast to no more tears for men, repeating what my mother used to say: crying for a man is wasting your tears. Our nights always ended in laughter, especially when Ursula would describe how she would dress up some of the patients and they would pretend they were going to the opera, listening, joining in and dancing to the music. What a delightful, creative nurse she was to those patients. How I admired her, her creativity, her love for those unfortunate people. She taught me to give of yourself, even when it is very difficult, and find in the other that spark of divinity that is in all of us. Those nights hold memories that continue to inspire me even after dust has accumulated on them... *la poussière*... dust that Bernanos says accumulates only when we become static or stagnant.

Through Ursula I met many French ladies and I never forget the marvelous lunches they gave. They offered gourmet foods, among which was a dessert called *île flottante*, the floating island, which became my favorite and I ordered it whenever we went to France. I remember one special occasion during a family trip to Paris when we had it at the restaurant Ledoyen, situated in Maria de Medici's house. It was an exquisite house with a wine cellar which we were shown when I told them I was Italian, and a menu that cost as much the entire trip. What an experience! Through Ursula I also met Marianna del Santo and her family, in Michigan, delightful people with whom I could speak Italian. The three of us became inseparable and enjoyed many activities together, likes picking apples in my garden and then making our specialties: la tarte aux pommes, apple strudel, apple sauce, and an international array of other delights.

Ursula and Licia, 1987

When Ursula left for Switzerland I cried like a baby, but fortunately my family and I visited her several times in Basel, and Leon was an indefatigable guide, taking us to the Alps and to see the glaciers. One visit to the Alps took place shortly after we arrived from southern Italy one hot July afternoon. We went to the top of the mountain by train and visited an ice cave; I in my Italian sandals, freezing my feet off and being photographed by Asian tourists laughing at the absurdity of my attire. A few days afterwards, we left for Vienna via train. What spectacular views! While admiring the surroundings I thought of my Ursula and how much she must have suffered, living first in Pontiac and then in Birmingham, which was more tolerable. What a brave and courageous being, my "Ursuletta" was and is.

During my knapsack trip to Europe, I met Ursula at the airport in Frankfurt, Germany, and from there we proceeded to Heidelberg, a delightful small, quaint town with interesting shops and restaurants; all of which we enjoyed very much, but most of all we loved being together. The next day we visited the famous Philosophers' Walk in honor of our Licia, who was getting her PhD in philosophy. We spent a lot of time there philosophizing about our lives, what different roads we had travelled and still travel, yet we were so harmonious with each other that it seemed as if we had come from the same place, molded by the same clay and sustained by the same breath. Each evening we would go to a different restaurant, and it never failed that Ursula would attract men dining there, who would send us glasses of exquisite wine. Ursula was most graceful in accepting their generosity and thanked them with her beautiful smile. What a wonderful time we had; laughter and joy became our companions. We left on different trains, Ursula for Basel, and I for Frankfurt to meet some of my students and their families, the Stegers and the Ghoussainis.

One spring we went to southern Italy for my cousin Gigi's wedding, and Ursula and Leon joined us for the celebration in Tropea, where she met my Zia Maria, who liked them very much and was able to speak some French with them. Ursula and Leon adapted well to the Calabrese way of doing things and very much enjoyed the festivities. I was delighted to see them in my milieu, which had the magic to transform me into a more joyful person.

Ursula and Marianna's family in Calabria

My relatives were proud to meet the Swiss couple who had come from so far to share this joyful event. They also met my Renda family (on my father's side) in Reggio, a beautiful city on the sea looking at Sicily across the straits, which stood there sprawled like a bear, dormant to the world until evening, when it awoke with its many lights, illuminating and exposing the many little villages and cities on the coast; a miracle that happened every night to the delight of the people in Reggio, taking their evening walk along the Corso, the main road along the seashore. My uncle Ottavio and his family took us to a restaurant by the sea not too far from Reggio, and there we were treated to a plethora of different fish, fresh from the sea and grilled to perfection by the master chefs at the restaurant. We ate, drank the local wine presented in clay carafes, made by the local expert potter's hand, and laughed, speaking French, English and Italian and using translations when necessary for our Licia. At one point in the evening Leon, the observant pediatrician, noted aloud that Licia and Ottaviuccio, Uncle Ottavio's grandson, both rolled their eyes occasionally, showing the white part, surmising that there was so much to see that they wanted to absorb it all. Ottaviuccio responded honestly that that may be the case with his cousin Licia, but for him it was more nervousness that he would stutter. What honesty in Ottaviuccio, what security and confidence he had to so generously disclose that part of himself. We were all touched and felt that this teenager will go far in life.

We met with Ursula and Leon again in Reggio for Ottaviuccio's wedding a few years later. They both enjoyed the wedding in a little church on a promontory overlooking the sea. What an idyllic place; Calabria is made up of idyllic places, each more charming than the other, under a magnificent blue sky and caressed by the sea which, with its perennial movement of the waves, constantly invites us to reflect on our lives. I am thankful to my Swiss friends for crossing their majestic Alps to my sea of beauty and love. I don't invite many people to visit my paradise, but they are among the few. Thank you, Ursula and Leon, for coming into my childhood world, a world that radiates warmth both for its brilliant sun and its people. I had not seen Ursula as radiant herself in any other place… a sun worshiper and a goddess of the sea.

3

Michigan Faces

FRAN HACKNEY

Fran is the first lady I met in the United States when I went to visit Thomas, my fiancé, who was then working at the attorney general's office in Lansing, Michigan, and sharing a house with Chuck Hackney, Fran's fiancé. How fortunate for me that we were both visiting at the same time; I liked her immediately, and as we got to know each other we discovered we had many things in common, both immigrants from Europe, Fran from Holland at age six, I from Italy at age seventeen. Fran was a social worker and had no difficulty conversing with new people. I, on the other hand, was rather shy and embarrassed about my accent and my provincialism.

Chuck and Fran came to our wedding in Toronto and we remained good friends ever since. I met her family, including her mother, a very impressive woman who had an elegance of stature and in dressing, with her slim and shapely body. I loved to see her whenever she came to visit from Holland. She brought me a breath of fresh air from Europe, a place I yearned for. Fran's two sisters were also tall and statuesque, and I visited them whenever they came to Lansing. Later, Fran's children and our Licia loved to play together, and they always came to Licia's birthday parties.

Chuck, Fran and Teresa at Licia's wedding, 2003

We had many wonderful dinners together at each other's houses, the last one at my house during the Christmas season shortly before Chuck was diagnosed with ALS. Chuck and Tom had a special relationship that began at the University of Michigan, where they both attended law school, and the diagnosis affected all of us deeply. Thomas kept in touch and would visit him most weekends and, as the disease progressed, would go and read to him.

Fran's kids, Steve, Tim and Susan, were devastated and tried their best to help their mother cope with it all. I felt for my Fran, who had a very difficult task both as a loving wife and as a mother, trying to comfort her children, keeping the household running, and interviewing health assistants to help care for Chuck, who needed twenty-four-hour care. I loved Chuck, a gentle, caring soul who came to see me in the hospital numerous times, to share our joy when Licia was born, and to comfort me during my many illnesses. Fran, too, was always there at my side whenever misfortunes struck, comforting me and sharing my pain. She made sure I had my fresh vegetables and fruits from the market, saying she bought big quantities and was willing to share them with me. Fran became my best friend, and we took trips together to Stratford, Ontario, to see some of Shakespeare's great works. We loved being together and sharing our passion for books and learning.

After our beloved Chuck passed, she managed to keep her family together by nurturing them and helped them from falling into despair, for her children loved and venerated their father, a real father who participated in their lives and took pride in whatever they did. Fran remained stoic and did not indulge in emotional outbursts; she had to keep her family afloat. What a strong and remarkable woman she was and is, always ready to give a helping hand. I love Fran very much and bless the day we met, for she inspired me and continues to do so to this day. Although I live in Boston now, Fran comes to visit at least once a year and we laugh, talk and enjoy good food.

What I admire most about Fran is her confidence, her truthfulness and honesty in every word she utters, and every counsel she gives—a frankness that is reassuring. She has an independent mind and is not easily influenced; she is authentic and generous but above all has a sense of justice. She is adventurous and loves to travel and share her experiences with those of us who can no longer do so. She is a life learner and I have learned a great deal from her: to be strong in adversity and seize the moment.

MARY KELLY

Mary was one of the mothers at the International School in Detroit, where I was the director, and where her children, Sally and Sasha, attended. Sally was the only student at the school who followed the French Curriculum as required in France. Sasha attended the French Immersion Program and learned French quite well, his mother supplementing the classroom with frequent trips to France. During one of these trips, Mary and the children visited the Musée d'Orsay, a marvel of Impressionist and Post-Impressionist collections, when a French lady approached Sasha, then an eight-year-old, and angrily complained that there were no paintings of Cézanne's. Sasha immediately answered that Cézanne was a Post-Impressionist artist and that his paintings were upstairs. The lady, amazed, asked where he was from. Detroit, he replied; and the lady, snobby and ignorant, left with an "affreus."

Mary and I became very close friends, and we still are. She inspires me to be good, kind and tolerant, a gift I cherish. We shared, and continue to share, our hardships, opening our hearts to each other's advice and comfort. Her balmy voice is soothing and refreshing to my spirit when I reach the limit of endurance. She inspired me when her first husband died rather suddenly, leaving her with two children, one in high school, the other still in elementary school. Her strength at the burial was colossal, her blond hair flowing in the wind and she holding her Sally... an indelible picture of sorrow and strength. She did not force Sasha to go to the funeral. But the day before, I took him out for lunch and there he wrote a letter to his father, concerned that he might make spelling mistakes. Mary inspired me to be a good and loving mother. Although still young, she did not want any men in her life at that time, and she dedicated every day to her children until they both graduated from college.

Mary Kelly at Licia's wedding, 2003

Eventually, she met Clyde Kelly, a tall, handsome man. I was the first to meet Clyde when we had dinner at my house with Janine, whom she loved like a mother, taking care of her and making sure she met all of us from the school. Mary had had a beautiful childhood in Iran; she was brought up like a princess, her father being in the government with the Shah of Iran. At the young age of ten, her father took her to a private school in England, where she learned English. After the Shah was deposed, Mary returned home, and at a very young age she married a doctor, and they emigrated to America. Hers was not a marriage made in heaven, but she remained a dutiful wife until the end.

What most impressed me about her was that after each setback, she reinvents herself. After she was widowed, she used her sewing skills to create evening purses of exquisite beauty, harmony and colors with old precious hardware; each unique in form, color and size, everything blending together to form a unique work of art. Then she decided to become the owner of a travel agency, a fruitful business until the crash of 2008, when she was forced to close and go work with a major travel agency, where she had to learn the language of new computers. She worked as hard as if it were her own enterprise. She also worked in the cardiology department of a doctor's office, again having to learn a new scientific language. What strength, what a mind. The agency she worked for closed its Michigan offices due to Covid, and Mary, once again, finds herself at a crossroads. She will never surrender and has decided to again own her own business, with her own clients who love her for her efficiency, patience and ability to solve their travel problems.

I feel very connected to Mary. We share the plight of immigrants, adapting to new customs and modus vivendi, but above all we share a childhood, each in separate parts of the world, different, yet very similar. Like me she loved animals and nature; she talks of her small pet donkey whom she cared for every summer in a little village she went to with her mother, where she lived an idyllic childhood. How brave she was, having been left in England by her father to attend private school and learn English at the tender age of ten, when separation from the family can be detrimental to one's psyche. But Mary overcame it all and she remained cheerful and understanding, without rancor.

What an admirable woman; I am blessed to have known and to know her, a teacher to me and a loving friend.

MARY REED

Mary Reed, the mother of one of my students, Sarah, a child with the bluest eyes I have ever seen, became another of my closest friends. I taught a series of cooking classes, and Mary came with some of her designer friends; we had a memorable time, cooking and then eating the food we made. Thomas joined us with some good Italian wine, an essential for an Italian dinner. She also participated with other mothers in my Italian classes, which I taught in front of the fire at home. What fun we had!

Mary impressed me with the love and dedication she gave to her scholarly brother, George, whom she raised, for her mother was confined to bed and a wheelchair due to a debilitating immune disease. After her mom died she took care of her father, a professor at the University of Michigan. Later, when George became incapacitated himself she moved to California to live near him. What a sister! What I found exceptional in Mary was the grace with which she gave her love. I wanted to be like her, suave, gentle, indefatigable, always ready to give a helping hand. Courageous, she left a husband and raised Sarah alone with the help of her loving family.

Mary understands me and my Latin roots. Her mother too was an immigrant, from Mexico, who left her family for an American husband. With Mary I can open my volcanic heart and let the lava flow out as she listens patiently without interrupting the flow. I learned from her not to interrupt and applied that with the children at school and with my daughter. I discovered that children would talk about their angst to adults more if we waited until they were finished and gave them advice only if they asked: "What do you think I should do?" Then they are more likely to heed our advice.

Mary is a continuous inspiration to me as we discuss books, children and our lives, which have not been too clement to us; although, with intelligence and strength, we have overcome many struggles. Every phone conversation is a joy for me, a treat in which I delight; I can never have enough of her. Her artistic flair is manifested in every move, in every word, in every texture she touches.

Mary Reed with her grandson Andrew

She is an interior architect and her sense of form and composition amazes me. I saw it in action when she took us to visit the Hearst Castle (Once known as La Cuesta Encantada, The Enchanted Hill) in San Simeon, on the Central Coast of California. She became our guide, pointing out the texture of many items, indicating the various elements that made the harmonious whole. The gardens were a visual treat, a blending of forms, sizes and colors, forming an enchanting whole that captivated our senses and our imaginations. With Mary I could see forms and an inner beauty in things natural and manmade, and a beauty in her own movements, especially in her hands, which enhanced her speech with even the least movement.

With Mary I could discuss any topic; books, which she read abundantly and voraciously; music, which she listened to constantly and studied through the saxophone. But the most remarkable thing we shared, and continue to share, is a good laugh, which often ended our conversations. To be able to laugh and cry with a friend is a great gift that a good solid friendship offers. I am blessed to have Mary in my life.

AURELIA TRANCHIDA

I was lying in Beaumont Hospital, in Royal Oak, Michigan, being administered a potent form of chemo to which my body reacted violently, and I had to be calmed down with Benadryl. As the nurses were reactivating the infusion, who arrives but my Aurelia, my dear friend who had just returned from Sicily to visit her family. As each dose was being administered, Aurelia knew the name of each one and which flower it came from; the blue liquid came from the blue myrtle flower, the red one, called Adriatica, came from the Adriatic coast in Italy, a rare flower that grows only there. She knew all this because she is an expert in botany. I closed my eyes and abandoned myself to imagination; flowers entering my body instead of poison, seeing the myrtle in my gardens, the red flowers near

Cattolica, the Italian beach we went to one summer, two years before my inoperable stomach cancer erupted. Aurelia's presence was so comforting that it left an indelible image in my brain.

Domenica and Aurelia at Licia's baby shower, 2004

I met Aurelia through my friend Domenica and I liked her immediately. With her calm countenance and depth of thinking, she was a quiet sort of person given more to listening than to talking, but when she spoke, pearls of wisdom came out. Everyone who met her admired and liked her. She was and still is married to Liborio Tranchida, a doctor in hematology who became my best adviser and counselor for my many medical needs. He visited me in the hospital when I had stomach cancer and told me that I was lucky to have the cancer then, for a year before, part of the chemo I was receiving, rituximab, was not available, and inoperable stomach cancer was lethal. Dr. Tranchida was very comforting and I felt blessed to be able to have had the treatment; what a close call I had.

Aurelia seemed to be there at the most auspicious moments. Like when we went for a walk in 2010, as we used to do in summer and autumn around my neighborhood, and suddenly, as we were climbing a hill, I passed out. Aurelia valiantly broke my fall, and I was unconscious for a short time. She left me in the care of a neighbor, who immediately came with cold water, while she went to my house nearby, got her car, and drove me home. We sat in the shade in my garden and both decided that I was overheated and had fainted.

I loved to see Aurelia, a very intelligent woman with whom I had many discussions on the difficulty of adapting as immigrants, on books, on philosophy, and on our children, who also became friends and went to France to study the language. Paul and Vincent, Aurelia's two children, are good human beings dedicating their lives to medicine and healing like their father. Since we moved to Boston, Aurelia continues to inspire me every time we talk on the telephone, both of us missing the great afternoons we spent in my gardens, which she loved and saw from their inception. She encourages me to carry on by the way she handles sorrow and misfortunes and transforms them into hopeful sonnets. She is a model for me with her profound love for her family, both in Michigan and in Italy, and how intently she listens before commenting, concisely and carefully. Aurelia is like a good book that resonates in your memory after the story ends. I am blessed she became a vital part of my journey.

MARIA VOZZA

I loved my International School, which I directed for many years, writing curricula, with a heavy emphasis on languages, music, art and art history, for international and American children from preschool to grade eight, with some students in high school. But I loved the end of the day, when on my way home, I visited Nonnina, Domenica's mother, who lived near our house and was always attending to her garden. She would fill a big bag with her delicacies and we would go inside, drink coffee and talk about the day. I loved to listen to her stories, which were like a reservoir, and she would pull them out as easily as one pulls water out of a well. But most of all I was fascinated by her war stories, which she narrated with voice inflections and emotions, reliving every moment. I was touched by her courage as she told me how she crossed enemy lines in Milan, transporting her beloved son Angelo to the hospital on a bicycle with a high fever. What courage, what love!

Our visits continued for many years, and Nonnina narrated another episode of her wartime years, when she and her family left Milan for Verdello, where they lived from 1942 to 1945, the end of the war. Verdello was a little holy town in the Bergamasco region, near where Pope Giovanni XXIII was born. In almost every family was a son who became a priest or monk, or a daughter who became a nun. The people of Verdello were very religious, and every morning the streets filled with the sound of their wooden sandals on their way to church. Almost every family in Italy was given bread rolls during the war, one per child. Nonnina received three bread rolls, one for each child, but she never ate them, a sacrifice that only loving mothers make. Verdello was part of the Padana plain, where there was heavy cultivation of a plant called "rape," whose minuscule yellow flowers were used to produce oil. For the natives of Verdello, these plants, which illuminated the fields with a sea of yellow, undulating in the wind, a symphony of colorful sounds, were inedible, but not to Nonnina, who would furtively go early in the morning and cut off some of the tops and then cook them for lunch. It would have been ideal for her to have had the boiled rape with a bun, but there were only three, one per child. If her son-in-law, Pino, who was not yet in the picture, were in charge of the distribution, Nonnina would have had bread with her rape. For the first time I understood why my own Nonna Dirce, also from Lombardy, would look at us strangely when we devoured this blessed vegetable.

    Nonnina told me many more stories, which I shall narrate another time. I cherished, then, these beautiful gifts

I brought home, together with the vegetables and lettuce from her garden, and I cherish the stories to this day.

Maria Vozza

DOMENICA PETRELLA

I loved to visit Domenica's house for her warmth and the sharing of her culinary talents, which greatly influenced my own cooking ability. Entering the culinary sanctuary of her house was an olfactory experience; she was always creating some masterpiece; even the simplest ingredients became glorious when cooked by my friend Domenica. Her focaccia and the Easter doves became delights in my family. She, like her mother, Maria Vozza, always sent me home with some of her creations.

I learned from her how to store partly cooked *la sfoglia* in the freezer to make lasagna and pizza crusts later, and many other delicacies. She knew which dishes were preferred by each grandchild and kept them ready for when they came. Her hands were strong and never stopped whenever she was in the kitchen. Her dedication to her children, Marisa, Patricia and Bruno, was inimitable. She would even dry fruits for her children's school lunches; her devotion was noteworthy, providing them with all the necessities of life.

Domenica, Teresa, pianist and Licia at Licia's concert

After her husband, Pino, retired he would make delicious espresso for Domenica and me, and we would spend delightful hours drinking the nectar of the gods, rendered more delicious by Domenica's sweets. Then Pino would delight us with one of his wonderful stories of his days in Petrella, where he was born and lived with his extensive family. Petrella is one of the many villages that graced our peninsula, villages that often remain unobserved in the history of the cosmos until human events there make faces pale and hard hearts tender. A little mountainous village away from the main roads in the southern part of the country, it became a beacon of hope, a refuge for many Jewish people escaping German persecutors. Petrella became an international village overnight, opening its doors to French, German, Hungarian and Polish Italians, all Jews who were trying to escape the malevolence of Hitler and Mussolini. These refugees were called the Internati, sent to the most remote Italian places, safe from the German madness of 1940–1945. The Internati were people who had committed no visible or palpable crime; their only offense for the Germans was being Jewish, a brilliant race, which, despite various persecutions, had reached a pinnacle wherever it went, but which now found itself in a minuscule point of the globe, surveilled night and day by the Italian police. Yes, Petrella was their refuge, but also a prison, surrounded by plains, mountains and rivers, churches and squares. The citizens of Petrella tried to do their best in sharing their meager meals. Among these people was a courageous fifteen-year-old boy, Pino, who worked at the city hall, the brains of the community.

Pino was an intelligent boy who knew how to type, a great gift during those times, and a great help to the police marshal, who knew how to read but not how to use the typewriter. Every document would go through Pino's hands, and he often helped the villagers.

But in times of war one needs more than typing, and Pino, slim but strong, also knew how to bicycle, which also became very useful. In Petrella, like many other places where agriculture was the main occupation, the flour mills were a source of life that suddenly became silent and unable to sing their ancient cantilena. The war had silenced them like it had done to those who did not want to accept the machinery of war. To rebel was not easy. Many people today criticize those who agreed to wear the black uniform; but to say no often meant death. Pino immediately understood that wearing the black shirt was not patriotic, but an acceptance of an evil that had enveloped the world in a mantle of black destruction.

My father, too, understood this and suffered the consequences by being beaten up by his own villagers for refusing to wear the black shirt. Every night after supper they appeared, dragged him to the river, beat him up and, after giving him castor oil, threw him in the river under a bridge, which months later, became the refuge of a woman giving birth to her seventh child, me. Years later I found out from my paternal grandmother that the reason the Blackshirts who tortured my father did not kill him was that they were the same people that my father had helped numerous times, building them houses, teaching them how to make coal, all vital for survival. And my grandmother had taught their wives to sew, how to raise the silkworm and make silk thread, all very common in the north where she lived her youth. She taught them how to knit sweaters and their children how to read and write. These men were the same men who would remove their hats as a sign of respect whenever they met my grandmother. The war, if one is not strong, makes even the angels malevolent, my grandmother would often say.

But let us return to Petrella, and the bicycle, where the war gave Pino opportunities to do good. Pino's uncle was an excellent mechanic and, knowing that the mills could no longer perform their daily work milling maize for the citizens dying of hunger, decided to go to the city hall and inform Pino that if the mayor was willing to procure him five liters of gasoline, he would be able to make the mills work again. The mayor asked Pino to type a letter and deliver it personally to the military commander in nearby Campobasso. Pino and Uncle Eugenio went by bicycle to deliver the letter. Campobasso was then under a Canadian commander, who thoroughly interrogated Pino about the proposed use for the gasoline, which he said would be used only to activate the mill. The following day two Canadian soldiers showed up with five big containers of gasoline and left, and soon Uncle Eugenio's ability began to manifest itself. He made a hole in the wall where the mill was, placed a tractor near the wall and connected the tractor to the mill with a belt. He then started the tractor and the mill immediately regained its voice. They sent a *bando*, an announcement, throughout Petrella that every family had the right to bring to the mill ten kilograms of wheat to be rendered into flour. Immediately people appeared like a brood of bee larvae in the honeycomb.

Every family in Petrella was given an Annonaria by the government, a registration document that entitled each family to receive flour, salt and other basic needs. Pino was in charge of the distribution, and now and then he would look the other way and give more to the many families who were most needy. The Annonarie papers were part of the monarchy's effort to help people during those difficult times. But let's go back to the years when the Germans were in nearby Limosano and the Internati from all over Europe were seeking refuge from persecution in Petrella. German soldiers would often go from village to village to surveil the people. The people of Petrella were afraid that the Germans would destroy their town and called all those with arms to the square, and ordered the others to stay at home. Pino's mother had four daughters, and she hid them away from the Germans in the attic. Sure enough, the German soldiers came from Limosano one day and stopped at Pino's house, where they found only the mother. She offered them wine, *salumi* and homemade crusty bread until they were drunk and satiated. Then they left for Limosano again, and in the dark of the night, probably drowned.

The Internati hid during the day, and in the evening they would come out to eat and get their mail, which was opened and read by the authorities before being delivered. Pino, generous and respectful, gave unopened letters to some he befriended. One of these Internati was a dentist who had a daughter with him. Pino thought of his own sisters and took pity on them. He invited them to his house to meet his mother and eat with them. The dentist noticed that Pino's mother had no teeth and promised to help her by making a denture, but he needed the tools and wires. Pino found wires and instruments that could be useful for the dentist. A month later he came to Pino's house with a denture made entirely of metal. The mother was very thankful, for now she could eat better. Again, Pino was of great help; kindness is often paid back with kindness. I often listened to Pino's stories, which made me thankful to have met him through his wife, Domenica. She must have heard them innumerable times, but she still listened as attentively as if she were hearing them for the first time, for she loved Pino very much.

Pino became very ill in the last years of his life, and Domenica kept him alive with dedication, love and good food. She inspired me to do the same with my mother when she came to live with us.

NYDIA QUIRORA

I spent a major part of my adult life teaching children, teenagers and adults English, Italian and French, writing curricula for the Canadian Citizenship Center under the guidance of Mr. Norman, principal of Rawlinson School, for immigrant children from the metropolitan Toronto area to learn English. I wrote a book series, *Il Grillo Parlante* (The Talking Cricket), for the Toronto Separate School Board, where I taught elementary and middle school, to commemorate the year of the child. I taught English grammar in the U.S. Army Education Center at Fort Knox, Kentucky, while my husband was stationed there. I taught Italian at the Evening College at Michigan State University and in evening classes at Birmingham Seaholm High School, as well as French at the International School, which I directed and for whom I wrote the curricula.

I met Nydia in my evening Italian class at Seaholm, which she and her daughter Ana attended. The moment I saw them I became intrigued by their unique presence. Nydia had an accent with a Spanish cadence, but Ana, no accent, the King's English. Their vivid eyes revealed an awareness and palpable intelligence. I wanted to know more about them, and after the lesson we had a revealing conversation. Nydia was Colombian, a pathologist who became a psychiatrist to have more time to spend with her three children. Ana was in love with a young man in Italy and wanted to learn Italian. Needless to say, we became friends and spent lots of time together.

We spent a Christmas together at my house, with Nydia devastated by her neurosurgeon husband who had left her. We made her laugh with some of my mother's sayings regarding men, like "One pope dies and another is elected." I told Nydia the story of *Lysistrata*, in which the women of Greece locked themselves in the temple and deprived their husbands of sexual favors until they stopped fighting, which they did. Women together can be quite powerful, and most of Nydia's friends, together with their husbands in the medical field, repudiated Antonio, her husband. I also told her the story of my grandfather Luigi, whom the women of the village punished by refusing his advances after his jubilation over his wife's death.

Nydia was, and is, a remarkable woman whose courageous spirit led her to very daring activities. Her inner strength helped her heal from an automobile accident that left her unable to walk and every bone in her body broken. With the help of her daughter, Maria, taking her to hot baths and many other therapies, she was able to heal and a few years later became a yoga instructor, showing her students difficult poses that made me cry for joy. Nydia became my muse, my guide through my numerous illnesses, always encouraging me to move on, not only with words, for words seem at times unable to express the depths of one's feelings, but with actions, her actions in moving on and dealing with excruciating pain. She wrote me a beautiful letter and gave me permission to print it here.

Teresa
My Italian teacher
My Inspiration for the search of health and life

To my dear Teresa:

Around 1982, when we met under unusual circumstances, I never thought that you would become so meaningful in my life. I began Italian lessons at Birmingham Seaholm High School, looking to expand my linguistic abilities. I knew very little of the Italian language; my background in Spanish was helpful, but nevertheless I began with a humble attitude toward a new endeavor. I was at the beginning of my career as a psychiatrist, and in the midst of raising my three children (Ana, fifteen, Maria, twelve, and Tony, nine). I enjoyed my Italian class very much, taught by a

Calabrese lady. She was full of happiness, full of zest for life. Learning was easy, although I had little time to study, but I had tapes, songs, books (her *Grillo Parlante*), and before I knew it, I could speak well enough to communicate with people in Florence and Taranto, where we visited Ana's friend. My children went "Italian crazy," Tony with Italian cars, *le macchinine*, Maria with traveling and Ana immersed in a fifteen-year-old first romance; their hearts filled with joy.

Years later, for some unknown reason, I learned about Teresa's struggle with carcinoma of the breast since age twenty-nine, when her daughter Licia was a still a baby. I thought, what a wonderful man she has for a spouse—he consistently provided unconditional support, love, and faith. Life continued on for Teresa in light of this diagnosis. The big scars were there but she remained beautiful and full of life. I love her for being a survivor and an Italian; she is like my family. I loved her for singing opera; plus we share the same motherly love for our daughters, and I loved her for her love for my daughter Ana, who could share her dreams and sorrow with Teresa. Today Ana is a pathologist living in San Francisco.

My friendship with Teresa went through many unfortunate changes in my life: travels, accidents, humble periods, moves; nevertheless, we always found each other. Last winter she was my "listener"—she had the patience to hear my latest tragedy, the loss of my health due to a car accident. I wore neck and hand braces in addition to cushions for back pain. Teresa and her husband were the first ones to hear about the loss of my husband of thirty-one years, deserting me because of my bitterness and pain resulting from the accident. I share my sadness but not my tears, for I have learned to live resisting pain and desertion.

My own diagnosis of breast pathology was suddenly awakened when I recalled that, during my forties, four breast biopsies had already been taken. These tests removed three-quarters of my tissue and distinctly scarred me. I experienced terrible pain, coldness, fear of losing my adolescence and of dying from polyps still growing... but I survived. My "third-world country" background seems to have come in handy when pain and despair strike by surprise. My medical school, pathology, and psychiatry experience did not do much for a woman in her forties suffering from the fear of cancer. Reportedly, one in eight women is surrounded by death and mutilation, yet so many remain uncertain and ignorant in cancer prevention.

My studies and my love for my women led me in a different direction: why? Why is it so predominant in the United States? This capitalistic society goes for the dollar, not the quality of food or cancer prevention, only for profit. Consequently we are sold contaminated chicken fed estrogen and chemicals, fish polluted by heavy metals, etc. I still had six calcifications in the breasts, and went to a diet of almonds, raisins, cranberries, blackberries, green and orange vegetables, fruits, soy milk, reduced my Lactaid to a minimum, and continued vitamins (C, B, A, D, E, Complex, Ca, Fe, Se, FnP, etc.), one every other day. A mammogram was repeated nine months later and the results were negative. I shared this experience with Teresa, and she suggested I write a note about my regimen for her book that deals with how to manage cancer while raising young children. I happily shared my experiences and my philosophy of life: meditation; exercise; no pollutants (alcohol, drugs, tobacco); a good low-fat diet, avoiding hormone-laden meats, and rich in vegetables. Treat yourself to vegetable masks on your face (cucumber, carrots, olive oil, tomatoes); go for Teresa's diet; change your tone in life: be positive; read poetry; embroider; knit; crochet; create gardens and look up and enjoy the immensity of the heavens, God's creation, nature and its beauty, the seasons, each laden with its own magic. Learn from my good Teresa that real life is a precious gift, that we go further and further for a reason.

Teresa and I had to meet to realize that surgery in

the seventies is not the solution of the nineties. The focus should be on preventing the illness through self-care: diet, lifestyle, etc. We need each other as collaborators, and the good universal force put us in touch through Italian classes. Teresa taught me, besides Italian, the zest for life that she emanates, and the fight against cancer in which we are partners forever.

I am indebted to Nydia for translating my first book, *For We Speak of Living*, into Spanish: *Hablemos de Vivir*. I love Nydia for her knowledge, which she gives freely, for her courage, for the love she has for women, but above all, for her thirst for learning, a true life learner. Meeting Nydia transformed me, resulting in stronger altruistic love, and a reverence for all creatures, big and small.

Teresa, Nydia and Tom

ELLEN MICKIEWICZ

I met Ellen through the Opera Guild in East Lansing, Michigan, in the mid-seventies; we immediately liked each other and developed a friendship that continues to this day. I immediately learned that we had many things in common: a love of opera, of Italy, where she took a sabbatical in Bologna, and a great appreciation of *la moda*, especially Italian designers. She loved to, and still does, dress well and with class, and with an elegance and demeanor not highly cultivated among university professors. She shone among the members of the Opera Guild like a bright star in the firmament, a star that enlightened my life at a very difficult juncture. Her charm, her intelligence and her warmth impressed and inspired me to be more like her. I learned a great deal from Ellen, who knew how to approach a subject and discuss it subtly and with finesse. She truly had mastered the art of conversation and discussion by listening, and then speaking; a lesson I was in need of learning, having a volcanic temperament and an upbringing in a village where everyone spoke at the same time; listening to no one but one's own voice, which rose in crescendos and then diminuendos like the sound of the sea that surrounded us.

Our families became friends, and Cyril and Licia, our beloved only children, often played together while we adults feasted on Italian food and Soave wine, which they introduced us to. We had wonderful times together but then had to say goodbye when we moved to Detroit and Thomas took a job with the federal court. I felt the loss but made a firm commitment to myself to keep in touch with this wonderful family, a great gift from the Opera Guild which, needless to say, stopped thriving when Ellen and her family moved soon after us.

Carmen, Britany, Teresa, Ellen, Melanie and Hilary at Licia's wedding, 2003

President Carter and Ellen

4

The Women in My Family

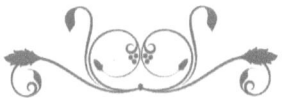

MY NOBLE GRANDMOTHERS, MARIANNA AND DIRCE

Two noble women, Dirce and Marianna, were the matriarchs who contributed to my DNA. One from the north, the other from the south, each spoke almost different languages, Dirce the language of Dante, Marianna the language of Capistrano, a dialect that was a mixture of Greek and Latin. I was not fortunate enough to meet Marianna, for she died rather young, when my mother was an adolescent, but I heard many stories from those who met her and esteemed her. The only girl in the family and an heir to a big fortune, she was convinced to marry Luigi Florio, an older man who did not love her, yet obliged by his tyrannical mother to marry the beautiful village girl. Despite their turbulent marriage, they managed to have a big family, my mother being the oldest of the girls. Marianna loved her brother

Carlo, who became a Bersagliere in the Italian army during the First World War and died in the north at the front. Marianna died leaving a one-year-old little boy among her children; how difficult that must have been for her. I feel deeply for this grandmother for I, too, was threatened with death at a young age, fearing to leave my eighteen-month-old child behind.

Painting of Marianna and Carlo

Marianna was a loving mother and tried to protect her children from the Spanish flu (which according to my mother lasted a couple of years, from 1918 to 1920), by taking them to her favorite orchard, where the children thrived in the fresh air and with the good food she cooked.

In the evening they would come home late, faces covered up to the nose by big handkerchiefs made by her. Marianna was very religious and attended Mass every morning before taking her brood to the country. Her husband was an atheist and a womanizer who felt liberated when his wife died, but something astonishing happened after her death. Every woman in the village that Luigi courted refused to have anything to do with him. They chastised him for having betrayed her, a gentle and honorable soul. The women of Capistrano, like the Greek women in the play *Lysistrata*, became the first feminists of Calabria.

Dirce was a loving grandmother to all of us children. She spoke Italian with a musical accent that entranced me like the Sirens did Ulysses, and I became glued to her. I was happy she came to Capistrano with her beloved Giuseppe, whom she loved dearly in spite of opposition from her father, who despised the southerners, telling her that oil and water do not mix. But Dirce disobeyed the paternal command and eloped. She was cultured and a born teacher, imparting to the people of the village her knowledge with care and patience. She became La Maestra, the teacher. She taught the children and the adults to read and write. Her house became a school in the evening for the adults who learned to sew, to cook, how to treat their children and how to cope with their authoritarian husbands. The entire village was captivated by this gentle creature sent to them from God, although she never accepted the Catholic Church and its abuses. She read the Bible discerningly, gleaning the good from the bad, the plausible from the implausible, and concentrating mainly on the Gospels and their wonderful stories, which she employed to teach reading and writing.

I loved my Nonna Dirce and would accompany her to the fields where she read to the workers from Dante's *Paradiso* while the poor souls ate their meager lunches. I once asked her why she bothered reading from one of the most difficult books in Italian literature, for the men surely did not understand. She stopped and told me that by hearing these beautiful, rhythmical verses, their spirits would be elevated from their daily morass. I remained speechless at the moment but pondered on her words for many years, learning a valuable lesson that there is more than understanding that forms a human being.

I was blessed to live closely to this giant and learn how to travel the road of suffering, abandonment and love. She crossed the Atlantic many times, the first trip with her family to San Paolo, Brazil, then back to Italy when she eloped with her beloved Giuseppe, only to return to Brazil again, after the birth of her son (my father) in Italy, at the invitation of her father. Unfortunately for her parents, her arrival in Brazil without the baby caused more consternation and unforgivingness, especially when they heard that Giuseppe's mother had run away with the baby an hour before Dirce and Giuseppe's departure for Brazil.

Giuseppe left Brazil, and the next day Dirce embarked alone, again crossing the tumultuous waters of the Atlantic.

How I admired this little woman who gave me a world of culture, art, literature, crafts and, above all, an understanding of childlike needs, which she fulfilled with love and tenderness. My trips to the fields with her to read inspiring texts to the workers during their lunch break remain indelibly set in my mind. How fortunate to have her in my young, formative years; the lessons of life she taught were stored in my being, ready to be pulled out during my many tempestuous adult years. A famous writer was once asked by an aspiring author during a lecture how one learns the art of writing. "Find an old woman and listen to what she says," he said. I was fortunate to have many such women in my family and village.

LA MIA ZIA ALBINA[*]

My Aunt Albina, so called because she was born at dawn, a true goddess of the dawn, would greet every morning when she got up to begin her long day of work in the fields, or preparing meals for the men who tilled and planted her fields, harvested the wheat and gathered her olives. I loved the wheat harvesting ritual, and as I have mentioned in previous books, it was an artistic event for

---

[*] See final chapter to read more about Zia Maria and Zia Albina, and others, in Italian.

me, watching the crows fly over the harvested land, diving down to eat the grains left behind by the thunderous thresher and by the children who became gleaners. Often the crows would get entangled in our voluminous black hair, and it was then that I learned to wear a kerchief around my head. When the church bells would announce noon, the tumultuous, boisterous machine would stop roaring, and we would all sit for a sumptuous meal laid on a big white tablecloth spread on the ground, under a big tree whose branches sheltered us from the hot rays of the July sun, *il sole leone* (the lion sun). My favorite dish was *pipi e patate* (fried peppers with potatoes), which my Zia Albina was a master at, accompanied by her crusty, rustic bread, worked by her powerful, small hands and cooked to perfection in her huge oven heated by the wood she gathered on her properties. She was a big landowner, who demanded her boys work in the fields with her, including my precious cousin Luigi, who had a palpable intelligence and memory, as well as a work ethic that distinguished him from the other boys in the family.

In church I would sit beside her. I loved when she sang during the Mass, her voice brilliant and strong, overpowering my faint, timid infantile voice. She was a strong, little woman in appearance, but inside had a soft, sensitive soul, which would manifest by the tears she often shed. I loved and revered my Zia Albina, who seemed to manage nature and man.

THE WOMEN IN MY FAMILY

Francesco (Albina's husband) and Albina

LA MIA SALVATRICE, ZIA MARIA

Aunt Maria was my comforter, and whenever I felt sad or troubled, which was often, I would go to her and empty my soul. I told her once about my angst and a newly discovered sorrow. She calmed me down, gave me a dried fig, sat near me and told me a story.

There was once a silkworm who decided to eat fewer mulberries and not become bloated. One night, when everyone was asleep in the house, she decided to leave the kitchen, where she was living in a big basket with hundreds of others eating away to death. A small gap in the kitchen window provided the exit. At first, she felt joyful to be in a bigger world with trees, gardens and flowers under a high blue vault. She loved the rain falling on her body, making her skin shiny, and the sun's warming rays gave her strength. She had never seen such a world; all she knew was being an egg, and then a larva eating herself to death. She was fortunate, she thought, but she felt alone in this world, where everyone else seemed to fit. Birds flew together, and butterflies frolicked together around flowers. But she had no one to communicate with; her species had chosen to follow a tradition that led to death. As she was slithering around, she lifted her head and saw a lady hanging colorful sheets in the sun, very fine clothing, which to her amazement, appeared to be the same as another lady was weaving on the loom. Could they have been the product of the silkworm cocoons? She thought and thought for a long time and became sad, thinking that she, too, might have become such splendid cloth. She had escaped from her duty as a silkworm and abandoned thousands of years of tradition, but for what purpose? To taste freedom. She realized that with freedom came responsibility; in her case, to live in loneliness, but also to savor the beauty of nature unknown to her; a variety of plants and trees, rivers and lakes, the refreshing rain, the open air, the warmth of the sun, all under the glorious vault of a blue sky.

I am happy I heard that story, for it made me think of the millions of immigrants leaving their cocoons for other countries, where, yes, they found work and opportunities to improve their lot, but they also suffered loneliness, discrimination and exploitation. To escape one's destiny is a monumental undertaking, full of regrets and hardships. *Chi lascia la via vecchia per la nuova, sa quello che lascia ma non quello che trova*, a proverb on the lips of every villager. (He who leaves the old road for the new, knows what he leaves behind but not what lies ahead.)

After I finished writing the story of the silkworm, as told to me by my Aunt Maria, I asked myself why that particular story was cemented in my memory, and I came up with a few reasons. Could it be that my aunt in her consciousness anticipated my leaving Capistrano (my newly discovered sorrow)? And could it be that I was that silkworm who escaped her destiny for an unknown world? Perhaps the silkworm is every immigrant who lives between sighing and acceptance, sighing every time the homeland comes into view, yet accepting the new world that can also offer moments of joy. Life is a road that each of us must travel, a road that eventually leads to the discovery of ourselves, of our soul, of our being.

Zia Maria and Teresa

THE MANY FACES OF WOMEN

Teresa and Zia Maria

Zia Maria and Teresa

5

My Immediate Family

Le cinque sorelle

NINA

"Five fingers of the same hand, you are for me," my father used to tell his girls whenever any one of us displayed anger toward the others. We learned from him to love one another, for in times of hardship we must draw comfort from one another. I experienced love and kindness from my sisters throughout my life. When I was born, my sister Nina, only twelve, carried me through the town begging the women with newborns to breastfeed me, for our mother was sick, and resorted to bartering, five minutes at the breast for a liter of oil. She became my little mother, protecting me and my sisters from the German soldiers who were camped in nearby Serra San Bruno, near a tunnel my father had dug to protect us from the bombs.

Nina was courageous and strong, defying the German soldiers who came to search our tunnel for the pilot of an American helicopter they had shot down. The Germans thought that there were probably no survivors from the helicopter crash, but my Nina, hearing the explosion, had gone and pulled the pilot out of the flames and dragged him to the tunnel, where my father had walled in a space for us to hide, if and when necessary.

The Germans came back and searched the tunnel, missing the walled-in subterfuge, and finding no evidence, pointed bayonets at us and began interrogating in German, with us not understanding a word. Our Nina stepped out of the line and told them in Italian that we knew nothing of the explosion and that our parents had gone to look for food. She spoke strongly and loudly, like a Roman emperor. I needed to go *pi-pi*, and I pulled the chamber pot out from under a bed and began to urinate, an act which spooked and repulsed the Germans, and they left. When we were sure they had gone, we went to help the poor pilot, who had been burned and was moaning quietly. Nina tore a sheet and began to bathe his wounds. When my parents arrived, after scolding Nina for leaving the tunnel to help the pilot, they took care of him, applying herb complexes over his many wounds. In the meantime, my father went to the Americans, not too far away, and through an Italian prisoner of war as an interpreter, was able to tell the story and prepare a plan to have the pilot returned.

MY IMMEDIATE FAMILY

A few days passed and the pilot improved. My parents dressed him like a peasant woman and put him on a donkey, with Nina sitting in front, together with a few baskets of chicory and dandelions. My mother walked behind, my father in front, leading the donkey. They were able to get through the German lines undetected, and were subsequently rewarded by the Americans with chocolates. Upon returning, Mother sat on the donkey with Nina, who was so happy that she had saved the American pilot.

We loved the American soldiers. They were young, kind, and had crossed the ocean to come and save us. They were our liberators from the scourge of the forties; and besides, they always carried chocolates in their pockets, which they shared with us. Many years later, in 1968, at Fort Knox, Kentucky, where my husband was stationed, we went to the PX and found the same chocolates I had received as a toddler. My eyes welled with tears as I saw those young soldiers, laughing and talking loudly, and I got lost in my recollections. Some of them were perhaps the grandchildren of those valiant soldiers who saved us, at whom the villagers of my town would throw flower petals as they chanted: "The gods from across the ocean who came to save us."

My Nina was always there for me, comforting and uplifting my spirits when I was down with my diagnosis and mastectomy for breast cancer at age twenty-nine.

When I went to Toronto to visit my family, she immediately wanted to see my wound, embraced me and held me in her arms like when I was a child. She told all of us that they must have made a mistake at the lab, for there was no breast cancer history in our family. She prepared a great meal for all of us and she stressed there was no cancer in me, and said we should eat and celebrate. I felt reassured, even though I knew the doctors were right and that I had cancer in my body.

Then we went to see a childhood friend who was not well, and had been in bed for a few weeks. Nina examined her belly after she said she had a tumor, and not feeling anything, she pulled our friend's blankets off and told her to get up, wash up and eat. Apparently, a neighbor lady had been flirting with her husband and convinced her that she had a tumor in order to come to the house, where she could see the husband, and use the excuse of bringing her broth and taking care of her. Nina went home and cooked a good steak and brought it to our friend. "Mangia se no non ti alzi dal letto" (Eat, otherwise you do not get up from bed). What power our Nina had. She even willed her own death after she lost her beautiful granddaughter, Rita. She had survived two open heart surgeries, but could not accept the death of Rita; she lost the will to exist.

MY IMMEDIATE FAMILY

Nina

THE MANY FACES OF WOMEN

Frank, Gina, Nina and Rocco, wedding in Toronto

Gina, Mother Renda, Ottavia and Nina

PINA

Our Pina was the index finger of my father's hand. She was so beautiful, delicate and talented, making beautiful silk clothes for us. She would embroider mine, creating beautiful fruits and flowers on the border, on the sleeves, on the front; I felt like a garden when I wore my clothes. She once had a boyfriend who bought her a curling iron. It was heated on live charcoal and she needed a victim to try it on. I was the chosen one. She would create a big curl in the center of my head, which made me the object of ridicule from the boys, but I held my head high, knowing proudly that I had something unique. She loved to unravel the silk cocoons, visualizing what our Nina would weave at the loom. I watched the whole process, the lifespan of the silkworm, and was astonished to see that at the end there were no silkworms inside. I asked where the silkworms went. Foolish questions, my sisters said. They had no patience or time for such nonsense, but my Ottavia, the middle finger of my father's hand, had the patience of Job and the kindness of a saint. She thought about the question and gently told me that the silkworm had entombed herself in the silk she wove with her saliva. But it did not make sense to me that the worm would cause her own death by disappearing into the filaments of the silk threads. I left the room and went out to ponder this absurdity, and with a heavy heart I ran upstairs to my Zia Maria, who enlightened me with a story. (See Zia Maria's episode, above.)

Our Pina was a jewel. She had golden hands that embroidered the sheets and pillowcases for our trousseaus; she sewed all our dresses, our intricate *verginelle* white silk dresses adorned with appliqués of cut flowers, all in white. She made the little purses where we kept our rosaries and the occasional candy. Her generosity was not limited to her family but extended to other children, whose parents worked from morning to night in the fields to scratch out a living. She refused to go to the country and plant or gather vegetables. Rather, she loved to go to the vineyards to harvest grapes, and to cook delicious food for us all for the festivals. She chose her household activities and was the queen bee, whom everyone respected for her talents. She was a real artist. When Princess Diana got married, she stayed up all night in Montreal to reproduce the princess dress, which was the first to hang on a mannequin in the window of the atelier where she worked. She made wedding dresses for all of us, including our nieces and many Montrealers who could not afford to buy one.

In Montreal, where she ended up, she and her husband bought a farm and transformed it into a paradise. It had fruit trees of every kind, grapevines, and cultivated fields of vegetables with a myriad of different beans which, when dried, supplied all the proteins in the winter. She made mozzarellas and other cheeses of every kind and taste.

MY IMMEDIATE FAMILY

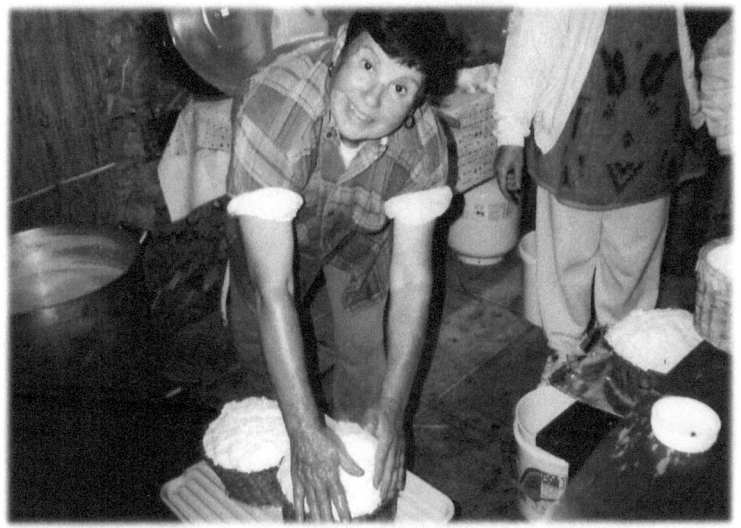

Pina making cheese

When I went to see her I asked myself where she had acquired such skills, when in Italy she had dedicated herself to the finer creations. What impressed me was the entrance to the farm, a long corridor flanked with hundreds of sunflowers that undulated their beautiful heads in the breeze, a celestial vision. Grapevines, with beautiful bunches of white and purple, formed a protective canopy to the ambulatory beings that passed through. It presented an image of beauty and harmony, created on a piece of barren land that had been full of weeds and thorns. The transformative power of our Pina never ceased to amaze us. She was a real creative spirit.

Pina, Teresa and Gina

Ottavia, Teresa, Gina, Pina and Mother Renda

One of the great gifts my Pina gave me was her son, Joseph. He went by the name Pino, and I loved him from the first time I saw him, when my mother and I visited them in Montreal. Pino was an amazing little boy, handsome, funny and loving. I made sure I visited him often, and would invite him to our home in Michigan, where we went cherry picking and enjoyed taking walks together. He developed into a young man bearing many of my father's features, tall, lanky, thin and with a smile that enchanted all the young girls. When he came to Toronto with his fiancée, my mother had a chance to talk with her privately, with me as a translator, warning her that handsome men come with a price; they love many and are faithful to none. She drew this conclusion from her own experiences. After they left, our Pina announced that the fiancée had left her son thanks to her prayers to Saint Joseph. My mother, in her wisdom, made no comments, and only laughed.

Joseph

Mother Angela, Bruno, Joseph

Unfortunately, Pino developed prostate cancer in early 2000, and after a valiant struggle, succumbed to the illness in 2007. But before he left us, I had memorable times with him. During chemotherapy, he visited me in my garden in midsummer, taking the arduous trip with his girlfriend, who had taken him to Niagara Falls on the way to

Michigan. I was working in the yard when I turned my head, and there was my Pino with his radiant smile, saying that he wanted to see me in my gardens. What strength, what vitality were still in him.

Later, one evening in January, I received a call from his eldest son, Anthony, saying that his dad was dying and was asking for me. Thomas scrambled to get me a flight to Montreal while I was busy making taralli, his favorite cookie. They cooked in time for me to take them to the airport, where I packed them in my big purse and perfumed the whole plane. When I arrived at Saint Joseph Hospital, I found the whole family there: his three children, the ex-wife, his father, sisters and brothers, uncles and aunts, cousins and many others. He revived when he saw me and asked me to take him to the roof of the hospital. I put my fur coat on his shoulders and we went like a procession. The nurses were beside themselves, loudly proclaiming in French that the Italians were crazy, but we did not pay any attention to them and continued. Once on the roof of the hospital, Pino asked for a last cigarette, and he smoked it with such pleasure that it brought tears to our eyes but satisfaction to our hearts.

We descended to the floor his room was on, and as we veered toward it, Pino commanded us to take him to the coffee bar on the first floor, much to the consternation of the nurses still babbling in French. At the cafe, he ordered cappuccinos for all of us, and smelled the taralli, which I took out of the bag and gave to him. He broke them into pieces and gave them to all of us to eat with the cappuccino, after which he told us a few things he had learned in his short life. He said to remember that when you fall down, you should get up and continue on living, no matter how many times life kicks you down, for life is worth fighting for by living every minute. All teary-eyed, we proceeded to his room in a procession to see him close his eyes forever. Now I understood why my sister Pina died shortly before him. She had stopped keeping doctors' appointments, despite a severe liver disease, because she definitely could not witness what we did, the death of her son, a loving giant.

OTTAVIA

Ottavia was the middle finger of the hand. She was tall, with black hair and shining black eyes that glistened, especially when her tears descended like stars. I was very close to Ottavia, who had the patience to teach me how to sew buttons, draw flowers and do many other crafts that helped me throughout my life. She was an excellent seamstress with talent and vision. She loved to draw in her spare time, especially the trees in springtime, when the blossoms enlivened the trees emerging from their wintery dormancy. I watched her for hours and collected her creations and saved them as treasures. All the boys of the village fell in love with her, as well as a gentleman from the north who came to Calabria to rebuild the bridges destroyed during the war. He saw her statuesque body leaning at the fountain where she went to fetch water and was immediately fascinated by her. My father heard about the encounter (nothing in Capistrano remained secret), and he insisted that my sister not meet the young man again, saying that northerners are not to be trusted because they come to the villages to seduce young girls. Was my father repeating the prejudice of his grandfather Leonzio towards Giuseppe, the southerner who eloped with his daughter Dirce? Then it was a northerner who did not trust the southerners. Now it was a southerner, Dirce's son, my father, who distrusted the northerners. What a crazy world, I thought; when will we learn from history?

Our Ottavia was compliant and obeyed my father's decree. But I did not remain silent like the rest and confronted my father, telling him that he had forgotten the story of his own parents and how much suffering such an edict caused them. He ordered me to be silent, saying I was too young to understand. But I resolved to be of help once I knew that Ottavia loved the young man, and I made myself available as her messenger. The young man was madly in love with Ottavia, and he pleaded with my father to let him marry her, but my father remained inflexible. When I met with the young man again I suggested that they should elope, but Ottavia did not want to. I suggested that he might reenact *Il Ratto di Polissena* (the kidnapping of Polissena), a tradition in some parts of the north, but he later confirmed that he loved her too much to do that. After my father left for Canada, Ottavia decided to marry a man from Capistrano who resided in Australia. She had never met him, but her sewing friends, who were leaving for Australia, convinced her to emigrate. When the young man heard this, he wrote in a letter to my father that he will never see his daughter again, a prophecy that came true. My father died in Toronto before Ottavia ever came back for a visit.

When my husband and I visited her in the late nineties, I was very happy to see her content with her four children and a husband who loved her very much. Angela, her younger daughter, and Peter, her Australian husband, took us through the eucalyptus forest, to see the koalas nestled in the trees, on our way to see the Twelve Apostles, primordial rock statues coming up from the ocean, looking like sentinels guarding the shore. I could not stop staring at them. Ottavia's youngest son took us to an island to watch the penguins come home at night. What a marvel, a spectacle of a natural ritual that occurred every night at sunset. We sat on benches amid the penguins' mounds, hearing the young ones quacking, waiting for their parents, who would recognize them by their voices. Our eyes were glued to the beach, watching the penguins advancing toward the shore like an army. First arrived the leader, then the others, forming a line, and once they were all out of the water the march began, always in formation, up toward the hill, to their young, who emanated a chorus of voices, each unique in timbre and volume and ready to be fed upon the dutiful parents' return. Nature never ceases to amaze us. We visited the museum in Melbourne, and I was enchanted by the detailed order of the design, as if each point was part of a story told by the Aborigines, drawing in the sand the many parts of their historical voyage through the forest and erasing it when all the members of the tribe had read it. Talk about living the moment! I bought a vase carved out of a piece of wood now extinct, a marvel of a sculpture. I cherish it and often hold it in my hands to admire its beauty, its reddish color and its form.

In Melbourne also lived my cousin Vince with his family. Vince is Zia Albina's first son, a jolly fellow with a big smile like his mom. He knew most of the people of Capistrano who had emigrated to Australia, and he invited many of them to his farm for a picnic. What a splendid afternoon we had, eating, drinking and singing operas and folk songs, with a tarantella here and there. Pina, Vince's wife, a real Capistranese beauty, prepared many of our favorite foods, including the famous *pipi e patati*. Being with my sister, cousins and family gave me great joy. Vince made a movie, which we showed later in Capistrano at my painter cousin Carlo's house.

Outside Melbourne, we visited my sister and her husband Raffaele's farm, right on the ocean, with a charming house, where I first saw the magpies celebrated in Gioachino Rossini's opera *The Thieving Magpie*, and I began humming the melodies. Raffaele had planted a copious garden and I loved the fresh produce. Ottavia and I would walk on the beach, talking and talking, for we had many years to catch up on. I loved being with her. We reminisced about our childhood and her decision to move far away to Australia to punish my father for having denied her her first love. How sad it was that we lived under a paternal rule, which often proved not advantageous to the ruled. I thought of the poet Kahlil Gibran, who in his book *The Prophet*, talks about the relationship between parents and children:

> Your children are not your children...
> They come through you but not from you...

My husband and I very much wanted to visit Sydney, a city of many splendors, dominated by Victorian architecture and the Opera House, built on the ocean in the form of a ship. My Thomas and I went to see the opera *La Bohème*, by Puccini. I thought of Mastro Antonio, the old man back in Capistrano who first introduced me to opera, and I wished he were there with us. Afterwards, we visited the famous restaurant dedicated to Mozart and had a lovely meal. My sister Ottavia and her daughter Maria, who came with us, went sightseeing. We met at the Queen Victoria market, where I bought the most exquisite linen clothes, a work of art in both design and unusual colors. We walked through the public gardens, where we experienced a rain forest, plants of every species, size and color, and a lovely space where old men were playing with life-size chess pieces. At noon a food truck came with food for the homeless and the poor, who were congregated in a special part of the gardens, with cheerful furniture upon which to eat their meals served in beautiful trays and surrounded by vast water lily pools. What a civilized world Australia had become since its founding as a prisoner colony. We visited where Captain Cook landed the first boat with the first batch of prisoners.

After three magnificent days we said goodbye and each took our respective flights, Ottavia and Maria back to Melbourne, my Thomas and I for Japan, where we would experience another new world. I again felt the pain of being separated from Ottavia; a month with her had restored our closeness.

After our visit to Australia, Ottavia visited my mother in Toronto and then came to the United States. What joy we felt when she arrived; what sadness when she left. Life is a series of hellos and goodbyes, of joys and sadness. I learned through the years to adapt and concentrate on the good moments, on those days of sunshine that are offered us to dispel the heavy clouds. How wonderful it was during that visit, when we all went to Montreal for one of our Pina's children's wedding. We had not all been together since the fifties, when our Ottavia left home for her long, exhausting voyage through the Pacific. No one had been there then to hold her hand when the waves played havoc; how brave she was, how courageous at such a young age, and for what? We sat together at the wedding, our mother among us, beaming with joy. She told me later that she became whole again, being with all her five daughters, and I felt her joy. She had suffered greatly to see her girls leave the nest for faraway lands she knew nothing about. In spite of all the diatribes life places on our plate, although mysterious, it is still beautiful.

Ottavia, Teresa and Tom

THE MANY FACES OF WOMEN

Ottavia and Licia

GINA

Our Gina was the fourth finger on my father's hand, the closest to me in age, and was my jewel, the rose in my garden. We grew up together and spent most of our days as children playing together. We worked side by side gathering olives in the winter, and searching for chestnuts after a windy night of brutal winds would have shaken the majestic chestnut tree, dropping the chestnuts into the grass below. What a thrill to find one, I attributing the find to her, she to me. Gina was the news announcer of the town, knowing everything that happened in the village and reporting to us. Sometimes our parents would intervene, if someone needed help. Gina was one of the most generous human beings in the village, sharing a piece of bread with other children less fortunate. She was generous also with her time and her money. The few pennies she made by running errands for some of the village women, like fetching water from the fountain, or watching their children when they went to the river to wash clothes, were always available. Her generosity was her mission. In

Gina

Toronto as a young mother she worked hard to provide a better life for her six children. She was constantly cooking, providing her family, and even the old ladies who lived on her street, with delicious meals.

She worked in a pastry shop and learned how to make the most beautiful cakes, cookies and biscotti, which she perfected in taste and shape. She would never let anyone leave her house without a bag of biscotti of some kind. She canned tomatoes for sisters, cousins and everyone she knew. We would go to Toronto for a visit and come back with hundreds of jars of tomato sauce. What an ordeal it was at the border to pass all the various foods through. When my Licia got her PhD in Toronto, Gina made a banquet for all of us, including Thomas's parents, who had come for the occasion, driving all the way from Muskegon, Michigan. Her home was always joyful.

Gina and Mother Renda at Gina's house

When I had my first mastectomy she suffered a great deal, and went to buy beautiful materials to make me a wardrobe adapted to my new physical needs. What generosity! One of the employees in her food market told me that without Gina's help with money and food she would not have survived the many hardships of her life. Our Gina was the most loving person I know. She loved everyone, deserving and undeserving; she gave generously without judgement, just like the apple tree we saw in our Pina's orchard during our trip together to Montreal.

Gina, on Pina's Montreal farm

Unfortunately our Gina left us when still young, barely sixty. I was there beside her when she took her last breath, gently, softly and with great ease. Her heart, healthy and strong, kept beating for a while, a golden heart full of love for everyone she knew. And she would have known many in the procession, in front of her casket, which continued for two evenings and one day. Gina's death was like that of a saint, eyes looking upward, as if visions from above were guiding her journey. Her stillness would silence my tongue. Her eyes, closed forever to the sunlight, would open mine to the light of love, by her examples of living in the Now. Most of us live suspended between the agonies of the past and the anxiety of the future. I shall live in the Now, in this moment, in the temporary darkness her last breath left me in. I stood there holding her hand until all the warmth was gone and rigor mortis began to set in, slowly, creeping like a weed around a flower. Her soul was traveling, some say, through a dark tunnel toward the light. My mind, still in shock, could not accept that my Gina was gone, and I indulged in visiting another "tunnel," a dark, windowless room in a small house in the village where all five of us girls slept in three single beds. How we loved that room—dark, big, cavernous, a huge womb where we slept, talked, played and fell out of the narrow beds. The light from the oil lamp played on the white walls and gave way to our imagination. We inhabited places with turrets, drawbridges and beautiful gardens, but we always came back to our cavern, where solemnly stood, in a niche in the wall, a huge clay jug, containing the most precious gift God gave us... the extra virgin olive oil that savored our meals, making even the most unsavory vegetables like dandelions palatable. The oil in that jug was magic, like dew refreshing the morning air, making every dish shine with glee, irresistible to young growing bodies. Olive oil was the nectar of our existence, and like bees with their honey, we cherished it.

Of course it took a long process to become oil. Gina and I loved the metamorphosis of those little white blossoms becoming our sustenance. We watched the process every year, beginning in summer, when the trees were full of blossoms, raining down upon us and emanating an orange-like scent. We felt like nymphs, dancing and singing, as the sweet scent descended upon our garlanded heads. Nymphs of the olive trees, whose long branches bent down to the earth, protecting us from the bombs of the cruel Second World War until the Angels of Paradise, the Americans, came to rescue us. We were happy to see their helicopters spray us with DDT to clear the lice from our heads, even though the day after the heavy spraying, the helicopter came back throwing down papers saying to keep children inside. Too late, for we had already been damaged. My Gina took her last breath from an autoimmune disease and many of us also later suffered from compromised immune systems. I have often wondered if it was the DDT that caused those problems.

TERESA (ME)

I was the little finger in my father's hand and became his favorite. He loved to listen to my stories, my fantasies, my poetry recitation and opera singing. He was very musical and played the clarinet or guitar in the winter evenings in front of the fire. How I loved those musical soirées, especially when Mastro Antonio came to teach us opera. I hung on every word, every sound he uttered, and when he hummed the "Anvil Chorus" from Verdi's *Il Trovatore*, my father played the triangle. After the maestro left, my father would play the guitar and Uncle Carmelo would play the mandolin, both instruments made by Zio Carmelo. I could not get enough of their music and I adored those evenings, especially the winter nights, with chestnuts roasting in the fire and munching on them all evening.

Later, in 1967, when I returned to Italy for the first time, I was looking through papers and found a letter addressed to my father announcing that I had won a singing contest run through Maestro Orlando and inviting me to attend one of the conservatories in Calabria free of charge. I was angry that my father never told me about it. He knew how much I loved opera, but I guess he was afraid of losing me to music.

I loved my sisters and, as the youngest, became their postman, delivering letters from their admirers. I also played many tricks on them; especially during the feast of Saints Peter and Paul, at the end of June, when lovers sent small bouquets to their beloved with lovely notes hidden among the flowers. I would stop in the fields, capture crickets and put them in the bouquets before delivering them. As my sisters smelled the scent of lavender, orange blossoms and jasmine, the crickets would jump out, startling them. Needless to say, they did not trust me to deliver flowers anymore.

As I looked deeply into my family's travels, it stood out to me that mine was a family of immigrants, dating back to the nineteenth century, crossing oceans to reach faraway destinations. I was struck that the common thread seemed to be the ocean, be it the Pacific or the Atlantic. My great-grandparents Martinelli, residents of a little town near Mantova, left at the end of the 1800s for Brazil with their numerous children. One of those children, Dirce, my grandmother, fell in love in Brazil with Giuseppe Renda, a southern Italian who had also immigrated to Brazil. Since northerners and southerners do not mix, according to Dirce's father, Leonzio, they eloped back to Capistrano, Giuseppe's village.

My grandfather Luigi Florio, about the same time the Martinellis went to Brazil, left for California, landing in New York at Ellis Island, where he is still registered. He then left for California in search of gold during the gold rush, joining a group of cowboys with whom he would stay until his mother tricked him into returning home, claiming she was dying. My beloved Pina left Italy for Montreal to be with her husband Toto, and soon after that my father, Fineo Renda, immigrated to Montreal, via New York, sailing on the Andrea Doria during her last safe crossing. Soon after, my sister Ottavia left for Australia to be with her husband Raffaele. A long perilous voyage. My beloved Nina left for Toronto to be with her husband Rocco, and soon after that my beloved Gina left for Canada as decreed by my father.

The ocean became my enemy, carrying away my family. What misery I felt, how lonely and empty my existence became. When I turned seventeen my father decided that it was time for my mother and me to join him. This was a shock, knowing that I, too, would now have to cross the hated ocean and land in Halifax. It was a tormenting voyage, with gigantic waves threatening my existence. I thought of my many ancestors, especially my grandmother Dirce, who crossed the Atlantic several times, and tears streamed down my face. Why have we all been called by the tumultuous ocean; for what purpose did it inflict such pain on our souls? A mystery for the Oracle at Delphi to solve.

MY IMMEDIATE FAMILY

Licia and Tersa, Lake of the Hills, after Teresa's first surgery

Mother Renda, Teresa, Licia and Mother Carlson,
home from hospital after first surgery

THE MANY FACES OF WOMEN

Teresa at the park after radiation, 1972

Licia, Teresa and chorus girls, *Carmen*

MY IMMEDIATE FAMILY

Licia and Teresa with Gypsy chorus girls, *Carmen*

Licia, Teresa and Louanne, *Carmen*

International School student and Teresa, Mardi Gras

THE MANY FACES OF WOMEN

Teresa in Okemos house

Licia, Teresa and Mother Renda, Okemos, 1978

Tom's swearing-in ceremony, 1979

MY IMMEDIATE FAMILY

Tom's swearing-in ceremony

Teresa with grandson Julian in her Japanese garden, Detroit

6

The Ladies, My Special Teachers

GERTRUDE CARLSON

Gertrude with baby Tom

THE LADIES, MY SPECIAL TEACHERS

Gertrude Carlson was my husband's mother, who soon became mine too. Most people have problems with their mothers-in-law. I, instead, was blessed with a loving, gentle, artistic and caring lady. I was most happy when she would come to visit or we went to her house, which mirrored her tremendous taste, class and artistry. She was a true artist and loved china painting, specializing in roses, which in their impressionistic beauty seemed to come out of the china plates and deposit themselves in your hands. I loved to go to her house and admire its beauty and harmony, each object, each piece of furniture, chosen with utmost class. She loved the Queen Anne dining room style and would always have a bouquet of wild Queen Anne's lace flowers in the center of the table. I learned a lot from this magnificent soul: how to appreciate fine china, crystals, silver and paintings, which she collected during her trips to Europe with her husband, who could never do enough for her, so great was his love for this small, dainty woman.

Enzo and Gertrude in her studio

I came from an environment quite the opposite; no fine china in our humble house in Toronto, no beautiful furniture to grace the old house, an immigrant home where survival was the business of the day. As I got to know the Carlsons, I realized how differently my husband and I were in our upbringing; I, struggling to survive in a small village during a savage war, he, brought up like a little prince eating Cheerios and watching cartoons. Yet our love was so strong that it overcame any differences... *amor omnia vincit*; love conquers all.

Mother Carlson was with me during the joyous time when our Licia was born; when she finally had a little girl, who not only looked like her as a baby but was a welcomed change from raising three little boys. She was there during our hard times, when life was tenuous for me, and promised she would help. Thomas would always raise our precious Licia if the worst were to happen. She was the most comforting and helpful mother to me. Both she and Father Carlson participated in most of the events of Licia's life, including her violin recital at Vassar College and her graduations from Vassar and the University of Toronto, where she received her PhD in philosophy. Their eyes were beaming with pleasure and pride. How blessed I was to have a second set of parents who loved me like a daughter, a daughter they never had.

THE LADIES, MY SPECIAL TEACHERS

Grandparents Carlson and Licia at her concert to benefit school

The Carlsons, Licia, Tom and Teresa at the Carlsons'

OUR ANGELA, MY NIECE

Gina and I did not give birth to our niece Angela, our sister Nina's eldest daughter, but our love for her was not unlike a mother's. While we still lived at home in Toronto, we would bring her into bed with us at night, after our Nina had the first signs of heart disease. We could not wait to get home in the evening to be with our baby, cuddle and kiss her profusely. As our baby grew we began to read to her, play games and teach her to read; she was not only beautiful but bright. She loved to play with other kids, always the teacher and the leader.

After Gina got married, Angela became my daughter and I felt like her mother. She followed me wherever I went, and my father said that she would follow me even into the confessional. After my father passed away, Angela continued to follow me and even meet my boyfriends. She became particularly attached to my friend Austin, who loved her and would bring her many wonderful books. At the age of eight she met my Thomas and became alarmed when she realized I was madly in love with him. She wrote Thomas, in the army, a very sweet letter telling him how much she liked him, but that she did not like the fact that he would take me away from Toronto. Angela suffered a lot when I got married; the saddest flower girl I had.

My marrying Thomas devastated many people in my family, and they all wished he were a Canadian living in

Toronto. My marriage was bittersweet, like the sugar-covered almonds at my wedding. I was ecstatic yet sad that I caused so much suffering. I had no idea before how central a figure I was in my family and how loved I was. Despite this realization, I felt like a rivulet that had to journey to join the greater sea and become immersed in the waves of love.

After my wedding, I kept in constant touch with my family, especially my Angela, who would write me the tenderest letters. After two years in the army in Kentucky, we returned to Michigan, and I had more opportunities to see Angela. In 1970, after the birth of my Licia, Angela came to spend some time with us and bond with her little sister; I had two daughters now. In the summer of 1972, after healing from my first mastectomy, we attended the Michigan Prosecutors' Convention on Mackinac Island, and we took Angela with us to help me with Licia. What fun; no cars on the island, only bicycles and horse-drawn carriages allowed. We visited a Native American settlement and chocolate-making houses and took many carriage rides. One day we rented bicycles and rode around the whole island, stopping to admire the sugar-sanded coast that glistened under the brilliant sun, and dip our feet in the crystalline clear waters of Lake Huron. In the evening we went to functions, where wine and cheese were served on the great balcony of the Grand Hotel, where we stayed. After the sumptuous dinner, there was music and dancing. Licia was enjoying herself, and I had my two daughters and my Thomas with me. I felt like I was in heaven.

Angela and Teresa on Mackinac Island

A few years later my Angela fell in love with Dominic, a charming, fun-loving young man, born in Toronto to Calabrese parents. We all went to their wedding and a beautiful Italian-style reception, with traditional food served over many courses and ending with a divine wedding cake made by an Italian bakery.

Dominic and Angela

Later in her marriage Angela had two daughters, Rita, and Nina, several years later.

Rita and Licia

When the girls were still young, Angela found cancerous cells in her breast, and for me began another Via Crucis (the Road of Sorrow) to see my Angela suffer so much. Thomas and I went to Toronto and saw her before surgery. The surgeon answered the many questions Thomas had written down, and he was confident that the surgery would go well. My beautiful Angela suffered a great deal with the chemotherapy that followed. Our Licia was studying in Toronto during that time and was able to be of some comfort to Angela.

Angela and Licia

I felt reassured that Licia and my sisters were there to comfort her, especially Gina, who loved Angela like a daughter.

Then in 2001, another tragedy befell our family. Rita tragically passed away in a fatal car accident. We all suffered immensely. I never forget the courage Dominic had to go upstairs into Nina's room and tell her that her sister had died. Even the rocks out in the garden cried.

After the loss of her beloved Rita, Angela became enveloped in a deep cloud and lost her way in the Dantesque forest, fighting the monster of loss for a decade or so. But her tenacity for life helped her to come out of that dark, ominous place and bring her back to the light, to her beloved Nina, now the only surviving daughter, who showed so much strength in dealing with her loss by immersing herself into playing hockey, a sport in which she excelled. Nina grew into a beautiful young woman, accepting everyone regardless of race or creed and unwilling to judge or condemn other people.

Palma's daughter Nina, Julian, and Angela's daughter Nina

THE LADIES, MY SPECIAL TEACHERS

Nina

Dominic, her father, dedicated himself to Nina and her pursuits. Nina became a great comfort to her parents, with her deep love for them and her indomitable sense of humor, which made them laugh and kept them laughing. But Dom and Angela's world would be suspended between tears and laughter; a world in which only those who had lost a child could know the depth of agony. I love this little family deeply and try to keep them close to my heart. Nina is a beauty, a work of living art; her beauty is endowed with strength and depth. One of my favorite pictures is of Nina playing pool, in which her pure Calabrese features shine through: olive-black, almond-shaped eyes, a Madonna face graced by thick black hair and the body of an athlete, agile and strong, never static, always in movement. I admire this strong and resilient family, a joy in my life.

Nina

Angela and I call each other often and visit either at my house or hers, with moments of joy that must be treasured and gathered to enlighten our long separation during these times of pandemic. I am blessed to have my Angela and my Licia, gifts from above. I could not have asked for more blessing in my girls, both loving, giving and caring.

Angela is an angel to many people. She has helped those who suffer from drug addiction, a neighborhood amputee, immigrants who are

Licia and Angela

lonely, and her own father, who is ninety years old and suffers from Parkinson's. She cooks, cleans and shops for him, even when she is in excruciating pain, often acting as his healing doctor. I have never seen such dedication toward a father.

Angela dedicated many years to working with challenged kids, giving them love and instruction. The children loved her in return, sometimes even not wanting to go home. To teach challenged children is not an easy task, but she was so creative with them that she could make their days fun. She was of great help to the other teachers, many of whom were younger than she and had not experienced the pain Angela had suffered. To understand others, especially the children and their parents, one must travel many miles on the road of life. Angela understood that and tried her best to give ideas of how to treat and help the children to the other teachers. During summer vacation many of the children asked their parents to take them to visit her.

I cherish the time I spent, and still spend, with my Angela and her family, who visited me often pre-Covid in my beautiful gardens in Michigan. I got to appreciate her through our voyage of tears and laughter, her inimitable courage through the many adversities that she encountered, her ability to find peace in a tumultuous voyage, her capacity to laugh again and continue her journey by demonstrating generosity toward those she met on her way, especially toward her daughter Nina, whom she loves dearly. To me she has been an inspiration and a great comfort. As George Bernanos said in his book *Joy*: "Nous sommes venus pour un moment, un moment de joie..." (WE CAME FOR A MOMENT, A MOMENT OF JOY). Angela is part of this moment of joy, together with my Licia and my Thomas.

Lilly, Angela and Teresa in Niagara Falls

DZINTRA UZULIS

I met Dzintra a few weeks after my arrival in Canada, in grade nine at Harbord Collegiate. She also lived on the next street over from mine. She was assigned to be with me all day in school for the whole scholastic year. What a

THE LADIES, MY SPECIAL TEACHERS

great choice. She was lively and communicative, even though I did not understand a word, not realizing at the time that I was being immersed in English. I couldn't wait to speak English so I could find out who this beautiful creature was, where she came from, and who her parents were. Later I learned she had Latvian parents and a brother who, many years later, would come to my wedding and take a lovely short film of the ceremony and reception on the beautiful grounds of Inn on the Park. What a gift he gave us.

Dzintra remained my friend and became part of my family, visiting often and indulging my nieces and nephew, Angela, Palmira and Michael, by bringing them crayons, colored pencils, books to draw in, and little books telling brief but delightful stories. The children treasured these gifts and looked forward to Dzintra's visits. They were angelic visits; she looked like an angel with her beautiful smile, which displayed pearly teeth, and her long, wavy blond hair, which twinkled like stars under the light of the sun. What a vision.

I learned a great deal from Dzintra, especially her sensitivity toward children. By bringing all those small gifts, pencils, paper, etc., she realized the needs of immigrant children, whose parents struggled to survive and had no money left after buying the necessities. What a great lesson I learned. Dzintra was an integral part of my life. She was there with me at a few school ceremonies when I received prizes, on our trip to Montreal and then to Quebec City, where we had the time of our life staying at Le Château Frontenac, the most celebrated hotel in Quebec. There we met two young men who showed us around Quebec City and its surroundings and took us to nice restaurants.

Dzintra at Château Frontenac, Quebec City

I learned to laugh a lot from my Dzintra and to be joyful in seizing every moment that life offered us. What a gift the secretary of Harbord Collegiate gave me by choosing Dzintra as my guide, who became part of my life, sharing the happy moments of my life, including my wedding, where she was the maid of honor. Thank you Dzintra for the inspiration you gave me throughout my life.

THE LADIES, MY SPECIAL TEACHERS

Dzintra and her husband at their son's wedding

RITA DENINO

Rita, Aunt Albina's daughter, and my cousin in Calabria, will be treated in Italian, at the end of the book.

Basilio and Rita, 50th anniversary party

THE MANY FACES OF WOMEN

Luigi, Rita and Basilio, 50th anniversary party

Julian, Licia, Basilio, Rita and Tom, 50th anniversary party

7

Two Faces from Boston

MARGARET (PEGGY) FRANK

Peggy

Peggy Frank, my son-in-law's mother, is an impressive woman, tall, statuesque and full of stories about her life as a mother, a therapist and an artist. Peggy traveled a great deal in her life, bicycling through Italy with a friend at age twenty in the fifties, hard times to visit Italy, with the postwar reconstruction going on. She joined the Peace Corps, which took her to various parts of the world, skied on the Alps and then in the U.S. with her two lovely boys, Nathaniel and Jeremiah. Most summers she spent at their house on Cape Cod, with her boys and friends, opening her house to many. There she saw patients as a social worker, painted and gardened, which she loved to do, creating gorgeous gardens to the delight of all of us who visited her. She is a generous spirit and a great reader, whose thirst for knowledge has made her a life learner.

Peggy was raised by two outstanding parents. Her father was a psychiatrist who was denied entrance to medical school at most institutions because he was Jewish. However, he was accepted at Fordham, a Catholic university, to which he remained faithful, establishing scholarships for needy medical students. That scholarship still exists, and Peggy still receives letters of appreciation to this day. Her mother was one of the first women to receive a PhD in economics from the Brookings Institution, and she went to New York to take up the cause for women working in the textile industries under terrible conditions. She was a pioneer in the women's labor movement, and wrote voluminously, donating all her writings to Cornell University. What a courageous and valiant lady; what an example for her daughter Peggy, who also gave herself, heart and soul, to defend women's causes. What a courageous lady Peggy was, to raise two outstanding young men as a single mother and maintain a successful career in social work. She traveled with her boys, skiing, swimming, around the country, a courageous mom who gave it all to her family in spite of hardships. I am blessed to have met her and to have her as part of my little family.

Before she fell and had to move into assisted living, we met together often, sharing wonderful foods both at her place in Newton, Massachusetts, and at ours in Lexington. Although confined to a wheelchair after her fall, her Jeremiah made sure she spent the holidays with us, as well as birthdays and Jewish festivities. Jeremiah takes excellent care of her, visiting her often during the week. We used to share a meal with her every Friday evening at the home for elders, which offers beautiful gardens and a variety of birds that come to Peggy's window, where a bird feeder is strategically placed. I loved to hear about her interesting life, full of adventures and fun.

Peggy and I shared many beautiful events, the most important of which was the wedding of our Jeremiah and Licia in Seattle, at a hotel overlooking the ocean. What an idyllic place and what a magical moment. Peggy gave a wonderful speech, and I sang the "Ave Maria." A sumptuous meal of fish and steak, surf and turf, followed the nuptial celebration in a great room that overlooked the ocean and provided a spectacular view of Seattle, an interesting city which we explored over the days following the wedding. A month later we had another interesting reception in Toronto, where my family lived and Licia had gone to graduate school. Peggy was a great participant at the reception and enjoyed meeting my family and friends of Licia's and ours.

Peggy, Jeremia and Mother Renda, reception in Toronto

Teresa and Peggy, reception in Toronto

A few years later we became grandparents to a beautiful boy, Julian, who became the joy of our lives. The two grandmothers were appropriately proud and joyful about Julian's intelligence and many other talents, which, of course, each claimed as coming from her side of the family.

Teresa, Julian and Peggy

I thank Peggy for raising two wonderful, sensitive, thoughtful and caring sons, Jeremiah and Nathaniel, who joined our little family, bringing joyful and memorable moments. Nathaniel has become a gourmet cook and a wine connoisseur, enlivening our celebrations.

I admire Peggy for her vast knowledge, which inspired me to continue learning, become a better listener and share my angsts. She is a marvelous woman, strong and courageous, having raised two boys as a single mother; she was a professional woman, a dean at Smith College, and later built a counseling practice in Newton. A remarkable woman, a loving mother and grandmother, a counselor and good friend to all fortunate enough to know her.

LELLA ALLEN

Lella

I met Lella through an acquaintance who lived near her in Lexington, Massachusetts, and invited me to her house for lunch. At the time, I was in mourning for the Japanese garden that I had left behind in Michigan, a product of my intense suffering after the death of my beautiful great-niece Rita, who left us the day before her eighteenth birthday. But there was a force inside me that pushed me to go to the luncheon, and there I met Lella; she had a distinctive Italian smile that welcomed me into her life. I was surprised to learn that she had passed summers throughout her entire childhood in Calabria, in a little town not too far from my village, with her cousins from the north and their Nonna, who had a sizable terrain on the other side of the river. I wanted to know more, and she described, in wonderful Italian, how the children took the train from Rome to Pizzo Calabro, a long but enjoyable trip, to descend upon their grandmother, where they spent the whole summer playing from morning until evening, when they would sit down to a tasty meal prepared by the skillful hands of Grandma. I immediately thought of the aria from the opera *Otello*, in which Desdemona describes the birds swooping down from the heights of the great rocks toward a sweet but languorous melody coming from the fountain below: "Scendean gli augelli in vol dai rupi cupi verso quel dolce canto e gli occhi suoi piangevan tanto tanto da intenerir le rupi...." (From the dark rocks the birds descended in flight toward that sweet singing, and her eyes shed many tears to sadden even the rocks...).

Lella and I share a magical and primitive wild land, its mountains, its monasteries, its rivers, which gave both of us many hours of investigation in their sweet, swift waters, with huge magnificent rocks to sit on for hours on end. It is a magical land, the land of the Sirens, who call us to the crystalline, green and blue limpid waters to listen to their ancient songs, which inspired even Ulysses and his mariners as they crossed the straits. It is the land of the sun, with its incredible sunsets reflecting itself in the waters of the sea, mirroring our souls. You cannot taste the beauty of Calabria, where the sea gives abundantly of its fruits to its inhabitants for hours of culinary pleasures, and be happy anywhere else. Lella and I keep many traditions alive and share our memories nostalgically whenever we meet, when our childhood emerges from our memory chambers to delight and sadden us. We share the love for our grandmothers, the matriarchs of the family, who kept everything running like an engine without laments, but had to constantly work hard. We love to get together in a cordial, Italian embrace, vowing never to keep apart from each other.

I love Lella and her hospitality. Her wisdom and spirituality never cease to inspire me. We met at the right time, when we both needed the comfort of each other's words and actions.

Lella, George, Rita, Luigi and Teresa

8

My Mother

TWO WEEKS WITH MY MOTHER (WRITTEN IN ITALIAN IN 2003)

It was 3:30 in the afternoon when the train entered the station, thirty minutes early, and I was delighted to have the time to calmly admire this marvelous city, Toronto, not knowing why. My mother must have already been at the window to see me exit the taxi, but I felt no remorse for delaying my arrival; mothers know how to wait.

How pleasant it was to breathe the fresh air of my city, even though its constant wind took my hat, which, freed from my head, ambulated among the deafening traffic. I did not run after it; any attempt to reclaim it was useless. It seemed like it, too, was in a hurry, perhaps to reach the Royal York Hotel, in flight with the sea of people running left and right, or crossing the street without paying attention to the cars that flew by like the wind. The hotel overlooked the train station, immobile and indifferent to its revolving doors in perpetual movement. That moment, immutable with the passage of time, was exactly what I saw on the evening of November 12, 1958, when I first arrived in Toronto. There it was, bathed in moonlight, that colossal hotel, dumb and impervious to my pain and to my joy; the pain of the immigrant who leaves her own land for the unknown; but the joy to embrace her father again. The luminous exterior of the building would become for me a reference point.

I, too, remained there, standing like a lamppost, looking at that crowd, a frenetic anthill speaking Portuguese, French, Spanish, Nigerian, English and who knows what else. I felt reborn in the harmonious world of sounds, even though it was a world caught up in a fury. How I missed this city of mine. We both grew up together; she into a modern metropolis, a mosaic comprising many parts, each different yet similar in the essence of life; I, a woman no longer tied to that small village situated in a valley between mountains and sea. We both grew out of our infancy of a provincialism typical of the fifties. That evening in November, bundled up in a shawl, I stepped onto the icy cold sidewalk, holding a cardboard carry-on after a brutal trip in an old ship, and a train that went *a passo di lumaca* (slow as a snail). There was a snowstorm that would make the teeth tremble even for those well dressed for it, and a wind that penetrated the bones. I lost my breath for a second, until I fell into the gigantic warm arms of my father. I realized then how much I had missed him. The ocean had separated us for many years, but the train station had reunited us. It welcomed us in its darkness, its cold, these lost *pellegrini* (pilgrims), onto its soil.

The taxi stops in front of my mother's house and leaves me on the sidewalk with my suitcase, carry-on, and a leather bag full of books. The taxi takes off like a whirlwind. Maybe he was ashamed for having gotten lost, unaware that I too was (re)discovering this vast city, no longer in its earlier state. I wanted to thank him and welcome him for I, too, as an immigrant, lose my way often, and our English, despite our diligence, will forever retain that delicious taste of another land. Our Toronto does not care about our accent, where we come from, where we live, or whether we speak English or not. She is a wise and good mother, welcoming us and making each of us part of the total, a true mosaic, each part different but indispensable to the composition and unity of the whole. Toronto is truly admirable. One need only look and they can find themselves in the smallness of the mosaic tile and yet in the immensity of this sacred land of Canada.

My mother is at the window, nose against the glass, hands in the air gesticulating, inviting me to hurry. She disappears and descends the stairs slowly and methodically. She is a small lady with white and gray hair, like the fog, minute eyes deep in her head, and a radiant smile. Her lips grace a vigorous face, her hands tremble but are still strong, and she has a vibrant voice that still knows how to

Mother Renda

give commands. "The taxi driver leaves you in a hurry like a damned man without offering to help you with the suitcases, *che canaglia* [what a brute]! Toronto is no longer the city that it was before opening its doors to all these immigrants." I was astounded to hear my mother's prejudice, not realizing that she too was part of what she called the unsavory people.

We remove our shoes, carrying them upstairs, together with the suitcases. "But what do you have in this suitcase! What a snail you are, you carry your whole house with you." Suitcase in hand, we go up the arduous staircase slowly, my mother still chanting her miserere. I keep climbing behind her, laden like a donkey. As we approach the top of the stairs, a well-known and pleasant smell invades my nostrils. We arrive at the top of the stairs and turn right into a big living room. There is the blue couch and big chair, both covered in plastic to fight against the dust that, as French writer George Bernanos says, invades us when we are no longer in motion. The room is as still as the night. We put the suitcases down on a white towel in a corner of the room and proceed to the bathroom to wash the bottom of our shoes, drying them with a white linen towel which is then put in the hall to dry and replaced by another white towel. "The city is dirty, we must not bring in what its roads offer." Immediately she offers me the slippers I have worn for the last forty years, slippers that have never seen the outside since they entered her house. Now I am ready to wash my hands and face, my mother supervising it all.

Now that the hands and face are clean we fall into an embrace, our faces barely touching each other; no excesses, for my mother is a true minimalist in every aspect of her life. We enter the kitchen, a small room with the minimum of furniture, only the indispensable, and dominated by a big window through which enters a sea of light. A rectangular table against the wall near the window is set with a white tablecloth, a little worn out by time and constant laundering with tons of bleach to render it whiter than the sunrays that dried it in Capistrano did; the same tablecloth that crossed the ocean with us in a cardboard suitcase. Nothing in that suitcase was thrown away, for everything speaks of joys, of anguishes and of interminable, meticulous work, of lives lived under different skies, in a Mediterranean world where joys and anguishes join, intersect, and then separate, but never fade away. Yes, this tablecloth has become a functional relic, trying to combat time and preserve another era.

The sun is still shining on that linen tablecloth and on my mother's white hair, making both whiter, more vibrant and content to still be alive and useful. The tablecloth laughs with glee for being alive, despite the many surgeries my mother performed on it, darning it carefully and delicately. Its has been a long life, even if the border hardly holds together the special stitching called "punto giorno," a delicate embroidery that could only be executed during the day, for it required more light than that of the candles that lit homes in the evenings. How long had it taken those little seeds to became this tablecloth? Plant them, take care of them, feed them and then gather them into bunches so they could be taken to the river, where the bunches of linen would remain in the water to mollify before the massacre began. I still see my mother bent over a gigantic white stone, a smaller stone in her right hand, intent on separating the fiber from the protecting stock, already rendered malleable by the precious waters of the river. What strength in those arms, in those small hands. I would suffer seeing her work so hard, and in my young head I could hear that linen plant crying out: *Leave me in peace; I want to keep my precious fiber. I don't care about your tablecloth.* My heart would beat fast for that poor plant, which had done nothing malevolent, only her duty as plant, born from a small seed in a small field surrounded by wildflowers, nourished by the same hands now intent on separating her from her life's task. She gave little blue flowers the children would take to their mothers. But my mother did not hear or think about the lamentation of the plant. She continued her work with every ounce of strength in her body, ferocious, as if the devil had come out of my catechism book and taken residence in her. I no longer liked my mother, and taken by fright, I would find refuge behind a ginestra bush full of scented yellow flowers, and dream of a better world.

Still in the kitchen, I lift up my eyes from that linen tablecloth and see my mother intent on beating up the cutlets to make them softer and thinner. I begin to laugh, but she continues her work with seriousness and strength. When everything is ready we begin to savor the fruits of her labor: cutlets served with peas, stuffed eggplants, broccoli rabe *affogati* (sautéed in olive oil and various spices), olives of every size and color, eaten with the marvelous bread she made. It is a mélange of colors and tastes typical of Mediterranean villages. A plate of various fresh fruits and an espresso complete our sumptuous supper. Then we each hurry to the sink to wash the dishes; my mother of course wins by pushing me aside to go and rest because traveling is tiring. With my mother we do not stay long at the table to waste time in conversation; work was calling and the kitchen needed to be put in order.

I sit back at the table and once more my eyes fall on that tablecloth, and I seem to hear that constant rhythm of the weaving frame, where my mother used to disappear every evening after supper. I would follow her like a faithful dog, sitting on a small chair to look at her just like I am doing now. Her atelier was a big room where the *telaio* (the weaving structure) occupied the greater part of the space. All those threads, ropes and combs suspended in the air seemed like a puppet stage, and every marionette had its precise part to recite. My mother was the director who knew her trade and her *telaio* well; with adroitness she would lift the lower part of the *telaio* with her left hand by moving the majestic comb, and with her right hand she would navigate the *navetta* (shuttle) among the threads, transporting the new threads. Swiftly, without losing a beat, she would change hands to catch the navigating *navetta*, and with the other hand would pull the big comb down to join the new threads to the others. She would lift the big comb with her right hand and with the left she would throw the *navetta* from left to right, and the procedure was repeated for hours on end in the light of the tremulous flame of the candle which, too, announced its tiredness. I never tired of looking at that *navetta* crossing the large mouth of the *telaio*, opening and closing with a precise rhythm, like a metronome. I imagined it at times like the mouth of a shark that had left its world of water to enter the world of the *telaio*, our world.

MY MOTHER

My mother is still at the sink washing the dishes. How precise and methodical she is, and how strong, given her advanced age of over ninety. Her small hands; how many tasks did they perform, never still: sewing our silk and linen dresses from the cloth she wove for us and our friends, and weaving cotton for sheets and wool for blankets for our trousseau, a custom that weighed heavily on the mother of little girls, one of the reasons that mothers cried when a baby girl was born. Her hands were those of a fairy, always busy, with little time to caress children or hug them or hold them close to her heart, which beat always stronger in her anguished chest. It took me a long time to understand and grasp her complexities, not until it was too late, on her deathbed, the two of us alone through the night, unable to communicate. (See the description of her death in book one of my *Oddyssey* trilogy.)

Her anguishes were many. Every time the bells rang in a minor key, announcing the death of someone in the village, she was always ready to give a hand, washing and dressing the corpses. I never could dispel from my mind how she once washed, dressed and laid in the coffin a sweet girl who had died of scarlet fever, a very infectious disease, asking us children to go to the fields and gather wildflowers to adorn her hands and head. I watched it all from a keyhole, how she gave her the last touch of preparedness by putting a white rosary made from little white pearls in her marmoreal hands. My mother came out of the house, a liter of alcohol and vinegar waiting for her, took all her clothes off and disinfected her body, then proceeded to burn the clothes she was wearing. I was not afraid of the scarlet fever, for my mom was not afraid, but displayed courage in front of all the other women who stood there like mannequins.

That evening, when we were all sitting in front of the brazier to keep warm and Nonno (my grandfather) was going on about his life with the cowboys, my mother was still sad for the little girl who had died from scarlet fever, and for her mother, now alone without anyone to comfort her. But her hands were busy, knitting a woolen garment for my Nonno, who had caught pneumonia, which attacked his lungs, while he was with the cowboys in North America. I would wonder in my little head how it was possible that pneumonia could last from 1890 to 1950. Maybe it was a particular disease, but I did not dare to ask anyone in the room. My mother's hands seemed not to care about my thoughts, busy as they were, doing their filial duty. She would give the appearance of listening, but in reality she was always immersed in the world of tomorrow, where a list of chores awaited her at the appearance of dawn.

The eggs of the silkworm needed to be put in a warm oven to hatch and awaken from their slumber. It was delicate work; too much heat would kill the eggs, not enough heat would have stopped the magical metamorphosis. There were no thermometers to measure the heat; you just had to feel the oven. We children were already on the mulberry trees gathering the precious leaves that would be eaten by the worms after they magically appeared from the warmed eggs. They would eat nonstop until, having eaten themselves almost to death, they would become white cocoons, and then placed back in the warm oven to soften the fiber from their sputum. The process of the silkworm becoming silk threads intrigued me very much, and I would watch the worms as they exuded a gelatinous substance that would enclose them in their tombs. I was enchanted by the miracle, yet saddened by their suicide, which gave me silk dresses. I felt indebted to them and would remain near them until their end. Poor little creatures; what had life dealt them, death in order to clothe others... me.

My mother's list still had many other chores, like a basket of clothes to be brought to the river and washed. Oh, that river. We children adored the river, jumping in the water like eels, then coming out, wet like dolphins, and running after the multicolored butterflies in the flowered fields. We would make crowns to adorn our heads with those flowers, while our mothers bent over big white stones, washing the clothes with the soap my mother had made the week before in a big cauldron. Then we would return to the village, the women walking straight as a cane to keep their equilibrium, like dancers, sweating a ton from the weight of the wet clothes, while we children in front jumped up and down like crickets. Once we arrived home, my mother would layer the wet clothes in a big clay pot and pour boiling water with ashes from our fires to disinfect and whiten them. I would watch her intently, deciding that tomorrow I would be more careful not to dirty my dress. But my resolution did not last long. The hills called me to dig up the rich brown clay to create the shepherds, the sheep, Mary, Joseph and baby Jesus, for the *presepe* (manger scene) at Christmas. After the hot sun would bake and dry the figures, I would paint them with the colors prepared by my mother from vegetables and fruits. She was a real chemist and knew how to make everything.

The small, smiling, yet tired eyes of my little old lady penetrate my soul and bring me to the present. The little kitchen is cleaned and shining for tomorrow's meals. Then with a sweet voice she tells me we should watch the Italian news on TV. The news is about the war in Afghanistan. My mother closes her eyes for a little, asking forgiveness for the sleep that overtakes her after supper. "Sono vecchia, la vecchiaia è una brutta bestia." (I am old, and old age is an ugly beast.) "Combattono ancora?" (Are they still fighting?) Her gaze is far away; who knows where she is going. Maybe she is thinking of the wars she lived through. Maybe her thoughts stopped at that moment of World War I when she, a little girl of five, was seated on her mother's lap, watching the tears flow from her black, limpid eyes, like two black olives kissed by the morning dew. She tried to stop them with her fingers before they touched her mother's rosy cheeks. Why was she crying? A colossal figure with a big hat decorated with feathers entered the room, gave my mother a kiss and said he would never see her again, and then left for the front, never to return again; our dear Uncle Carlo.

My mother returns to the present and says how ugly war is, that it robs us of our dear ones and leaves us with broken hearts. And with that she opens her eyes to the horrible spectacles of Afghan women running and holding their dear children, trying to find refuge from the brutality of the Taliban and the American bombs falling from the sky like torrents of rain. My mother once more closes her eyes, this time to hide her tears and entomb herself in a silence that perplexes me. Maybe she was thinking that, like the Afghan women she, too, had run from the Germans during World War II, toward nearby Serra San Bruno, in the dark, through the hills, with children hanging on to her skirt, crying and falling like leaves.

After a long and arduous crossing of the hills, they arrived at Serra San Bruno and found refuge near the abbey, asking for protection from the founder of the abbey, Saint Bruno. He, too, was a runaway, from France, then Rome, and found refuge and peace among the beech trees that stood there, tall and proud, to protect the saint under their shade from the scorching sun, the winds of autumn and the rains of winter. My father, with the help of friends, built a structure with the wood of the beech trees that had fallen over the years, a structure with a long tunnel underneath, where we would go when the bombs fell, on us and the trees, like ice balls during a storm.

My mother becomes so absorbed in her thoughts that she is immobile, mute and totally absent from the present. I sit closer to her and gently caress her face. She fixes her gaze on me and tightly holds my hand. "Che disastro sono le guerre, ci rubano a chi la vita, a chi la pace... Non ci sono vincitori, solo perdite, ogn'unono perde una parte di se stessi... senza voglia di continuare, tale è la disperazione e la devastazione dello spirito... Io non avevo alternative, avevo un'altra nel ventre e delle volte mi chiedevo come fare a portarla alla luce e perché? Per soffrire... cosa potevo offrirle... un mondo a sfacelo, un mondo di pene... un mondo dove anche I buoni diventavano cattivi per il troppo soffrire, ed I bambini continuavano a voter nascere nonostante la fame in questo mondo non mondo, un mondo da cane." (What a disaster wars are, they steal from some their lives, from others their peace... there are no victors, only losers; everyone loses a part of themselves... no will to continue; such was the desperation and devastation of the human spirit... I had no alternative, another baby in my womb, and often I would ask myself, how will I manage to bring her to the light and why? To suffer? What could I offer her? A world destroyed and in disarray, a world of suffering, a world where even the good ones became bad from too much suffering, but babies continued to be born, despite the hunger that consumed body and soul ... wanted to be born into this non-world, a dog's world.)

The fault was mine and that of all the other babies that wanted to be born. Not of the men who, deprived of everything else, would turn to sex to find relief and comfort. She could not blame the men, whom they needed to build shelters and hunt for food. They were useful; children were an impediment, needing food and care.

She says that we should go to the kitchen to drink a cup of tea, for the war never ends. We drink the tea from her flowery English bone cups, transparent to the light like her skin, now thin from age and overuse. A tarallo accompanies our herbal tea, with her saying that this time the taralli turned out the best, and she devours them as if it were her first time eating them. My mother knows how to grab the moment; she savors each morsel as if it were her last. The war is far from her thoughts now, and she celebrates our being together in her spotless kitchen. I have a strong desire to embrace her, but I dare not for she has a cold, which, for my mother, is like the plague, and she must refrain from touching anyone and must wash her hands every five minutes. For her, even old age is a contagious disease; no one can use her comb, for it is an old lady's and could cause hair loss if even I use it. Her hand towel is another relic of old age, untouchable and unavailable to any hands but hers. No one can approach her in bed and give her a good night kiss; her cavernous mouth, devoid of her denture, remains closed until morning, when the denture is reintroduced. She is very private and protective of her body.

My mother also has a particular philosophy when it comes to medicine. She believes that to fight diabetes, one need only eat lemons after ingesting chocolates filled with liquors before going to bed. In the morning she faithfully measures her blood sugar, and if it is normal, she says, see, lemons do work. Happy with the results, she makes a good cup of coffee and drinks it in bed. At precisely nine o'clock she eats breakfast, which consists of a bowl of cereal with milk, and then begins her work. She always says that she has no time. She is as busy as if she were young, even though she is ninety-three years old. She cleans her clothes with the same attention she gave them when she was young, praising modern accessories like the washer, but not dryers; they darken the clothes, so she hangs them outside in summer, in the basement in the winter. Her clothes are assaulted weekly with a generous amount of bleach, a blessing she says, and she cannot understand why people, including her grandchildren, complain today, when everything is rendered easier by machines. I try to help

MY MOTHER

her hang the clothes on white cords, they too being prey to the bleach, but she does not let me, saying that we young people are not attentive enough to the job, being used to the dryer. She brings in the clothes in a wicker basket, well folded and needing no ironing. She climbs the stairs like a deer, carefully but at a good pace, carrying her basket with both hands. I follow her, worrying that she might fall.

I switch gears and imagine her in the village coming back from the river, basket on her head, walking straight and agile like a reed. We children stop at the side of the road, gathering blackberries or raspberries and stringing them on a stalk of grass, or gathering mulberries fallen from mulberry trees in a little basket made with our little hands from wild grape leaves stitched together with small twigs. What fun. Back in the village, our Nonno, a centenarian, would say that we were loaded like mules. I would immediately run to the kitchen to see the silkworms who, after eating themselves to death, would become white cocoons ready to be transformed into silk thread. Every time that this metamorphosis took place, I would promise myself I would stay up all night to watch it happen, but I never did. My world was full of failures and joys.

Back to my mother, who, having survived the steep stairs, immediately puts the clothes in the drawers, and now it is time to eat a small lunch, punctually at twelve o'clock. After that, we take a brief *pisolino* and will then go to the doctor on College Street for a checkup. She tells me that she should not be bothered by this at her age, but that we will go today. After a long monologue, we are ready to leave the house. She is all dressed up with shiny black shoes, silk clothes, and a pair of black sunglasses, big and shiny like two diamonds. They had been worn by her late husband, my father, and were kept in a velvet case, protected by a small silk handkerchief. We walk down Montrose Avenue until we reach College Street, where my mother's life unfolds every day. We first stop by the bank to deposit her pension money, which she carries in a small silk bag pinned to her undergarments under her blouse. We cross College Street, and on the other side is La Grotta del Formaggio, a cheese shop that sells fresh mozzarella, fresh ricotta and prosciutto from Parma. Then we go to the bakery for a loaf of crusty bread, an espresso and a sweet. Loaded down, I think we are finished shopping, but oh no. We enter a butcher shop, and immediately the young butcher greets us and runs to the back to wash his hands with soap and water, for which he is rewarded with a big, approving smile from my mother. How demanding my little old lady is!

We leave everything on a chair in the butcher shop and walk to the clinic to see the doctor, whose office is full of people. No one makes an appointment; they all come in like rapacious birds whenever it is convenient for them.

After a thorough look around, my mother announces loudly that we will not be getting out of there soon, and proceeds to wipe her chair with a white handkerchief, ironed to perfection. She then sits until the receptionist calls her in to see the doctor, a cordial young man who asks her in dialect how she is feeling. It is dangerous to ask a simple question of my mother, who gives him a very complicated response. She rattles off a litany of problems, headaches on the right and on the left side, dizziness, stomach aches, poor hearing, etc. Finally, the doctor interrupts her, asking what medications she takes. She opens her black purse and pulls out a bottle of Maalox, which she calls "milok," and says "that's all." The doctor has difficulty keeping a serious face and continues to ask more questions. He asks when the headaches come, to which she responds, "Eh, whenever they want." When asked about her dizziness, she asks the doctor, in dialect, if he knows how one feels when drunk. When the doctor says that he doesn't drink, my mother opens her purse, pulls out a hundred-dollar bill, and puts it on his desk. Obviously thinking that a man who doesn't drink can't be much of a man, she says to me, "Iamuninda, stu miadicu non capisce nene." (Let's go, this doctor doesn't understand anything.) I ask the doctor to forgive us and we leave the room in a hurry.

Still on College Street, we go to the Chinese fruit market, where my mother meticulously chooses each fruit and bean pod. Then a few feet away we enter the Sicilian Bakery, where she insists that we not sit at the window, but at a dark table in the back, fearing that people might see us. She is a private person, admonishing me not to tell people what we ate or are going to eat, and not to make people jealous and cast the evil eye on us. Loaded like mules, with five or six plastic bags in each hand, breathing hard and in pain, we turn onto Beatrice Street and then onto Montrose. We finally reach our house, and the bags fall out of my hands, upon which my mother asks if I am too weak to climb the stairs.

The next morning, after the doctor visit, she comes down with a cold, which she attributes to the many microbes in the clinic full of people. She takes a deep breath and begins to scold me for convincing her to go to the doctor, saying we should leave her in peace for she wants to go anyway. She takes me by the hand to her bedroom, opens a drawer, and shows me a brand-new box containing the garments for her final departure: shoes by Bruno Magli, the leading designer in Italy, a blue silk dress with ornaments around the neckline and the sleeves, a black leather belt, bra, panties and undergarments, and a *panciera* (girdle). "Make sure they put my bra on," she says. "I don't want to meet our Lord with old clothes. I hope God will not be severe with me and accept me." I feel sad and yet reassured that she is not afraid of dying.

I remember the story my sister Nina told me about a

beautiful, sunny summer day, when our mother asked her and my sister Gina to accompany her to the funeral home near our house to pick out her coffin. She chose the coffin, the prayer cards, and asked the gentleman to show her the room where she would be laid out. The room was on the first floor, which had no windows, and Mother refused. The gentleman, perplexed, said that all the rooms had no windows, but she refused to accept any of them. Our Nina, who had little patience for my mother, asked her why it mattered that there were no windows, for she would not be aware of such things anyway. Mother calmly looked at her and told her that it mattered because her daughters, who were all suffering from one disease or another, needed fresh air. The gentleman then took them upstairs, where the windows could be opened. She wanted to make sure he was not lying to her, but did say, "Qui' si respira bene" (here we can breathe better). Our mother thought of everything. She even gave Nina an envelope of money to pay for a dinner at Bar Italia after the interment. I was touched by those stories, and tears streamed down my face.

I adore visiting my mother and entering her world, so full of details, routines and good food, which permeates the whole house, especially when she makes taralli, which in Capistrano are made for the feast of San Rocco. During that feast, breads are made in the form of body parts to offer the saint to heal the particular part of the body represented by the pastry. I am intoxicated by the smell and the memories of the feast, embrace her and kiss her with love. She tells me I have lost *il decato* (the sense of measure), with my excessive reactions to the taralli. Here in Canada one can make taralli whenever one wants; abundance fills our stomachs but makes us lose our soul, the spirit of tradition, the sense of waiting for that special moment in time when all our senses are satisfied. Waiting is not for Canadians; every desire can be satisfied instantly. "We have, indeed, all lost *il decato*, and have become consumers par excellence," Mother murmurs under her breath. She continues murmuring until her eyes begin to close for a *pisolino*, which is permitted for a lady in her nineties.

Between my mother and me there are no tensions, perhaps because I immerse myself totally into her world, without attempting to modify it, her world full of harmony, a furtive world for those who do not immerse themselves in it. I now understand how annoying it must be when elders are constantly admonished by family, especially for my mother, who survived two world wars, a pandemic in 1918 (La Spagnola), which killed innumerable people, and was now witnessing, even if through television, the war in Afghanistan. She lived and lives the tragedy and joys of two different worlds, but which are similar in suffering. How futile our admonitions to her as she navigates her world: be careful not to go out when it is cold, be careful not to fall, eat more proteins, less sugar. I learned to be quiet, perhaps because I, too, came to know profound sorrow at a young age, a sorrow which can destroy any value in life and transcend national confines.

My mother is the teacher, not I; only she has the right to admonish us. I am conscious of the right a mother has and impatiently wait that a crumb of her wisdom might rain on me. My mother is like a majestic oak tree that, beaten by the many tempests of living, knows how to bend its branches so they do not break, and patiently waits for the winds of ill fortune to subside, and for good weather, even if temporary, to return. I want to venerate this almost centennial tree. I give her the polite form of you, voi, when I address her. How grateful I am for my colossal tree. I admire it from every angle and find in its contorted limbs the beauty and harmony of a bonsai and the strength of the oak tree. How proud I am of her.

"Ah, the taralli, are they ready?" she asks, as she opens her minute eyes from her snooze. She is ready to be in motion. She goes to the other end of the house, into the living room, and looks out the bay window, giving a glance at her majestic oak tree, full of birds chirping away joyfully and flying from branch to branch with élan. "How beautiful the naked trees are, full of snow; they become lighter by relinquishing all their belongings, their leaves, so they feel lighter to meet the weight of the snow, which would have broken their branches with all the leaves on them," she says with a wise voice. "How wise are the trees, not like you, who carries the whole house in those suitcases; there is a lot we can learn from the trees," she continues. She looks out the window, the window which has become her line of communication with the outside world, for winter in Toronto is very long for the elderly. "We old people are like the bears; we hibernate," she whispers to herself. Like the oak tree in front of her window, she, too, has lightened her burdens. She is not interested in solving problems anymore, having solved so many during her long life. She has eliminated the layers of suffering acquired through having to raise her mother's big family after she died young, and then her own brood. Now all those layers have been eliminated by the wind, just like the leaves of her oak tree, revealing an authentic structure.

Here she is, in front of her window, immersed in a colloquy with her oak tree, fragile yet strong in her new reality, free as a bird to live and die when the time comes, without rancor. No more illusions that dull your brain, but the reality of the naked tree that is in front of her. Both are in their universe, no longer in need of scaffolding to sustain them and hide their beauty. Yes, my mother is complete; life has sculpted her, chiseling away the rough edges, and now, splendid, she shows herself to the light. Only one support remains, a cane on which she steadies herself as she travels through the long corridor of her house. Life is an amazing process of building and demolishing.

MY MOTHER

Tomorrow I will go back to Michigan. I shall miss my little old lady, with her white-gray hair, still beautiful legs, and eyes, deep in the sockets, that still see everything; with her open smile that enlightens her small round face, radiant with youthful skin not totally marred by age. She no longer has that veiled and mysterious smile of the young mother, that smile that did not reveal the many anguishes she felt, yet was always reassuring that everything would go well, even when our stomachs growled. I shall very much miss that face of a Madonna, high cheek bones, with no sign of wrinkles on that limpid skin. She is transparent, my little lady; she has eliminated all the protective masks she accumulated during her long life. Now she is serene, open to all, with no prejudices, no fears; a child who does not yet know evil, the anguish of being. I am thankful to see such a metamorphosis in her, but I fear that it is the metamorphosis of her silkworms.

Yet, I am thankful that I survived many of my diatribes to spend time with her, and particularly to have been with her in 2002 when her sun, our sun, disappeared, when I had to announce to her that our favorite Rita had been cruelly taken away. She emitted a primordial scream that obscured her luminous face. She continued her languorous cry, which became like the cantilena that the women of Capistrano softly sang as they accompanied the deceased to the cemetery, carrying on their heads a brazier with live coals that burned the incense that ascended toward heaven.

How many dead my mother had accompanied, and now she would accompany her Rita. She remained stoic at the funeral and interment, emitting anguished sighs from her cavernous chest with eyes full of tears. Under the extreme heat of July she still remained standing at the cemetery, asking Rita to come and take her, to bargain with the Lord, if necessary, because Rita knew how to speak well. We returned home exhausted. I asked her what she wanted for the *ricordino* (a prayer card distributed at the funeral). She looked in the Bible, but nothing satisfied her so she dictated something to me in her own words. I wrote the words down and placed them in the Bible, the daily companion to her solitude.

Two weeks had passed since my arrival in Toronto. Our visit came to an end and I left for my home, where Licia and Tom met me at the train station in Windsor. On the train I wrote the above account in Italian, which I later translated into English.

As I was finishing the translation, and after many years of the continued war in Afghanistan, I turned the television on to witness a new civil war, this time in the United States, which has been a "beacon of hope" for many immigrants who escaped other wars and found refuge here. It was terrifying to see the mob being incited to march to the Capitol Building in Washington, D.C., in January 2021, to a place suffused with the history of the laws and traditions sacred to the country. And incited not by a foreign power but by the commander-in-chief, the president, members of his family and his supporters, senators and representatives, all of whose intent was to overturn the legitimate 2020 presidential Electoral College votes. For a moment I thought I was back in Italy during Mussolini's reign of terror, of which my father was a victim. The president speaks and acts like Mussolini, surrounding himself with thugs and yes-men and -women who do his dirty work. The mob acted brutally, breaking windows and entering the sacred chambers, like enraged dogs unleashed by their master to do damage and kill.

9

Reflections from My Diary

LICIA, OUR DAUGHTER

I wrote some reflections in my diary on New Year's Eve, 1980:

What a joy my little Licia is! She is indeed a gift from above, who comforts me when I am sad, clarifies my thoughts when burdens are too heavy, and straightens my thinking when, in haste, I pass judgement on, or condemn, others. Indeed such a gift is a rare one.

As we both look at the nativity scene, my eyes are filled with beauty and wonderment. What peace its stillness evokes, what unity reigns in that simple abode; I could look at it forever with my Licia beside me. So many families lack that peace, that openness that the hands of Mary and Joseph portray; an openness which fears no disclosure of lingering secrets. I thought that in such openness, in such total nakedness, each member of the family gathers strength, a strength that eliminates roles, the necessity of wearing masks. Each member is free to be, to become, and to follow whatever journey they desire. No wonder so many earthly families fail.

January 24, 1980, was a day of reflection for me, as I was cleaning and cooking and waiting for my Licia to come back from school. We had moved to the Detroit area, where my husband had been appointed a federal magistrate, and Licia had left her previous elementary school in Okemos and her many friends and beloved teacher, Madame Pelosi. It was a difficult decision to have Licia change schools in the middle of the school year, and I felt our daughter's anguish. I felt her anguish and felt somewhat culpable; perhaps I should not have consented to the move. Being a teacher, maybe I should have known better. Yet the thought of family unity prevailed. If he had to travel from Lansing to Detroit, Thomas would miss us very much, and we him.

I took a break from my chores and looked around. Our house was on a large lot and I felt like I lived in an unpopulated resort, surrounded by majestic trees, four of which were dawn redwoods. There was a small apple orchard at the back of the property, and singing birds and splendid sunlight which made everything glow. I felt at peace as I recalled a French existentialist writer who said that as long as we do things "à la foi," we should have no regrets. ("À la foi" means in good faith.) I felt very much at peace in this abode, perhaps not as beautiful as the one we had built in Okemos, yet free from memories of the loss of my breasts, of insurmountable suffering and anxiety. Its big luminous windows connected me with the nature outside, which surrounded us on every side of the house.

Thomas came home full of joy and exuberance. Licia and I loved to see him come home, so much promise in our embraces, so much peace, so much hope that the worst was over. This was only a summer day in our lives, everything glowing with the promise of a better future. But will the depth of winter be far behind, with its storms and catharsis? I hoped we could go surfing forever without touching the depth of the ocean; my eternal hope.

Our living continued, enjoying the fire in the fireplace in the evenings, talking, reading, listening to music and preparing Licia for bed, our little night owl. I loved to read poetry, and one evening I was reading Gerard Manley Hopkins. One poem especially touched on my experience with cancer: "Spring and Death," in which Hopkins describes death as marking some flowers in spring, in their prime, so it can easily identify them at harvest time.

> It seemed so hard and dismal thing,
> Death, to mark them in the Spring.

I feel fortunate in some way that I, too, had been marked in spring, which gave me greater ardor for life and time, not wanting to lose any moment with our little Licia or chance to love her every day. For tomorrow was not assured. Yet, I feel some regrets for such a marking, which also made it difficult for me to abandon myself to the act of living without a tomorrow being ever present, and which affected the delicate and blessed peace that tried to reign among the three of us. I stepped out to feed the birds who were waiting for their supper. How peaceful and worry-free their lives are. I thought of the poem by Leopardi, "Il passero solitario" (the solitary sparrow), which I loved to read to my little linguist Licia. The poem describes the solitary sparrow that flies free in the country and sings of its liberty. ("Il passero solitario che spensierato se ne va per la campagna cantando e vivendo la sua liberta.")

Three-year-old Licia, 1973

Tom, Teresa and Licia, First Communion

January 1982

The three of us went to see the opera *Porgy and Bess*, a memorable performance, for which our friends Paolo and Franca Canovi joined us. They loved Licia and treated her like a young lady, with warmth and kindness. A fine evening we had, and upon our return home, inspired by Licia's demeanor at the opera, I decided to paint her portrait with words. Here she is painted by a mother's insight, framed by a mother's love:

Taller and more grown than last year, yet still exuberant and loving. Her slender body, her beautiful angelic face, decorated with a radiant smile that discloses a dimple, her elegant hands with long fingers, her posture and demeanor, all the work of an artistic hand. So much beauty, so much grace, so much talent, all blended in a veil of goodness and modesty. What lessons will I learn from such a divine gift? Each day it is as if a veil is removed from my eyes, disclosing a gift as she gently reteaches me many lessons of life, of how to live a more perfect one. One day in Toronto, as we were leaving my mother, watching us from the window, Licia felt my anguish. She gently took my hand and led me away, silently, to a cafe. She ordered a *granitine* (lemon ice) for us and then began to talk. "I know you are unhappy about leaving Grandmother, but she is not unhappy. I know that, for when I go away to school or to play with my friends and you stand at the window, I, too, think you are unhappy, but then I remember your words: 'I am so happy, Licia, that you are going to have a good time and lots of fun,' and I feel content. Grandmother is like you, happy that we are going back to our Papa." What wisdom in her words; her thoughts are clear and crystalline and expressed with kindness and love, not preachy.

Licia writes beautiful, profound and humorous stories, not unlike fables full of meaning, with a summary thought that teaches a lesson. She loves to read stories with social and moral content and investigations like the Nancy Drew series, *Flowers in the Attic*, and *Jonathan Livingston Seagull*. She reflects on what she reads, comparing Jonathan Livingston Seagull to Christ.

I have a feeling that she will incorporate music and psychiatry to help humanity. Her music studies are progressing very well, piano, flute and violin, and joining the Oakland Youth Symphony. Here, too, she displayed tremendous maturity. She arrived for the audition and saw all the contestants practicing away. I suggested that she open her case and join them, but she informed me that she felt confident and ready. At the end of the audition, I asked her how she felt and she answered, looking at me with her piercing eyes, "Well, Mother, if I get in I will be happy ... if I don't I will not be disappointed; I will just study harder next year and try again." She did get in, even though she was only eleven years old and the minimum requirement was supposed to be age thirteen.

The first concert was impressive. They played Brahms' "Hungarian Dances," the "Nutcracker Suite," "Adagio for Strings" by Corelli, and a few other pieces. Seeing my little Licia on the stage, among over a hundred orchestra members, brought tears to my eyes, tears of thankfulness for having survived my breast cancer. She looked glorious in her taffeta skirt, and her eyes beamed brilliantly, a true window to her pure soul. She had my father's gaze, especially when he played the clarinet for me.

Licia smiles a lot, with fullness, with depth, with certainty, now more than ever. Years ago her smile was more fragile; now it is stronger, more certain, as her hands glide on the piano, or her elegant fingers wrap the flute. She smiles when the violin is in tune and her hands glide on it, or when we drink tea together in front of the fire, or when the red candle flickers its light and trembles like the tremolo on the violin. Thomas joins us with a story by Edgar Allan Poe, and we listen to the expertise he displays in reading them with the right voice inflections. We are mesmerized and could listen to him read for hours. Licia and I cherish the moments when Thomas comes home and we spring on him like deer; and he in his lovely way greets us with pride and happiness to be home with his girls. We follow him into the bedroom, where he changes into more comfortable clothes as we talk up a storm.

Licia is blooming into a beauty. Thomas and I feel lucky to have had her before the storm hit us. I bow in thankfulness. Like the pine trees, I hope to protect our seedling from the rain and the winds with our branches of love and care, but not too much, so as not to obstruct the sun that will make her grow strong and independent. I look to Kahlil Gibran for guidance, the poet from Lebanon, especially his book *The Prophet*.

Licia and I loved to read Dario Fo in front of a roaring fire, the Nobel Prize winner who wrote many funny yet serious tales. One we especially liked was about pregnant mothers who become soldiers and begin training their babies to do military exercises in utero. How we laughed; yet underneath that laughter were enough unpleasant thoughts to feed an army. Nonetheless, we continued reading and laughing. We also read a play by the same author called *Defenestration of an Anarchist*, written before a real event (the throwing out of a window) occurred, for which Dario Fo was blamed. His was a great mind, recognized by the world but not by his own country of Italy; a sad personal story for our beloved author.

Our many trips with Licia created beautiful portraits of our family and friends, with unforgettable memories. The first trip I took with Licia, when she was four years old, was to Stevens Point, Wisconsin, by boat across Lake Michigan, with Joanie Iwasko and her four-year-old son, Nicky. Both children were learning violin, and this was a music camp where we met for a class with Mr. Suzuki from Japan, who had developed a special method to teach string instruments to young kids. We loved the surroundings and the school, full of enthusiastic kids carrying violin cases of every size, with their mothers, eyes beaming with pride. My battle with cancer seemed far away, until I heard Joanie telling another mother that she came to accompany me because I had not long to live. Granted, Joanie was not the most tactful person, yet her gratuitous comments really hurt me. I hoped my Licia did not hear them. We continued having fun, however, for every minute with my Licia was a gift for me.

The following year during winter break, the three of us traveled to Paris, to visit the city of enchantment. We had a memorable dinner at Ledoyen, a restaurant situated in a house that had belonged to Maria de Medici. We ate in great style, Licia and I crazily ordering all kinds of fancy crepes, while Thomas ordered a piece of boar, the chef's recommendation.

Licia at Ledoyen, Paris

Only later did Licia and I realize that all the dishes were super expensive, because our menus had no prices listed. Only Thomas's menu, the gentleman at the table, had the prices. Plus, everything was cash only, so Thomas had to go back to the hotel and change some traveler's checks. Meanwhile, we ladies were given a grand tour of the house and the immense wine cellar, after I told the maître d' that I was Italian.

Then we went to the cafe where the author signed the movie rights to *Jean de Florette* and *Manon of the Springs*, two movies we loved very much. What a historical city! The following week we went to the Opera House, for a modern rendition of *Mefistofele*, with the Dutch composer sitting in the front row. At one point in the opera, the tenor sings out, "I want to go home." The audience rudely responded, "me too" in French. Poor composer! The French can be rude and insensitive in general. When we visited Versailles, the French guide first explained how they guillotined Marie Antoinette, then, without losing a beat, she continued, showing the queen's handkerchiefs made of the finest lace. My Licia whispers to me: "First they kill her, then they show her personal things, how sad."

Another memorable trip was to Venice to celebrate our eighth wedding anniversary. Venice is one of Licia's favorite cities. It offered her those wonderful gondola rides, going under the Ponte dei Sospiri, a bridge that remained imprinted in her mind, as years later she chose a violin called Sospiro, built by a Florentine lady in the style of the Venetian School of violin making. In Venice we went to the Teatro la Fenice, where we saw *La Bohème*, and after the opera we ate at the restaurant outside the Opera House, delicious food with a bowl of figs floating in water. Figs are one of my favorite foods, and my family knew how to make me happy. Licia was beaming with joy. She shared all the nuances of our life with us.

We visited the Piazza San Marco, with its St. Mark's Basilica and the Doge's Palace, marveling at the incredible mosaics, each tile unique yet part of a whole. I felt like one of those millions of tiles, distinct, yet belonging to the human race, with its beauty and ugliness, its joys and sorrows, its victories and defeats. I was part of a whole, belonging to the universe, to the stardust that formed me and us. How wonderful to feel part of a whole, rather than an insignificant speck of sand in this vast universe of ours.

In the evenings we would sip coffee in the piazza, under the stars gazing at us from above, and listen to the various orchestras that played the music of the spheres around the square. My family knew what I needed to dispel the cumulous clouds of cancer.

The next day we took a boat to Murano, the island where glass was blown by skillful and artistic hands, creating colorful objects. I went crazy for the jewelry, made of glass beads of every color, shape and size, creating a harmony and elegance. I bought gifts for everyone; the best necklace I bought was for Janine, our blind friend, who held it in her hands like a relic, feeling its beauty.

We traveled a great deal with our Licia. One trip she and I took was to Switzerland, after landing in Milan and boarding a train that took us through the Alps, the magic Alps with its high pinnacles looking to the sky as if in prayer, while the train traveled at a mighty speed through the high mountains. The landscape was overwhelming to the eye, with little villages sputtered in the landscape of graceful hills and valleys. I felt I was traveling in the viscera of the earth, another womb holding me in it. It was exciting seeing our friends Ursula and Leon, who picked us up at the train station and took us to a restaurant on the Rhine for a sumptuous steak dinner au poivre. How lovely it was to be with our friends and their daughter Barbara, one of the most beautiful women, an artist, who was very kind to Licia and took her out to visit Basel. We went to the mountains, the crown jewel of Switzerland, and on a long excursion in the countryside, a marvel of nature.

After a beautiful week, we decided to take the night train back to Milan and proceed to southern Italy, a long but exciting trip ahead of us, so the couchettes were most welcomed. Licia occupied the bed above me and, exhausted, despite the energy of the young, we fell asleep secure in our bolted cabin. All of a sudden the train came to a sudden stop and we heard noise from the cabin next to us. My little Nancy Drew opened the curtain and saw two masked men run toward the exit, followed by a train attendant in pursuit of the robbers. Another attendant came to our cabin asking if we were okay. Licia told them in detail what she had seen and then asked: "What are you going to do about it, and what exactly happened, sir?" The man was amazed and then asked us for our passports. Licia refused, saying: "My dad said never to give anyone our passports, and he knows everything." The official left with a smile on his face, thinking the mother could not speak English. Licia was proud of her performance and decided to write a Nancy Drew–type story.

From Rome to Naples is a short ride, and there we changed trains, a *diretto*, for the town of Pizzo. As soon as we sat down, a train staff member brought me my purse, which in the commotion of Naples, I had left on the seat. Licia immediately commented that, while Neapolitans have a bad reputation, someone had found the purse, gave it to the conductor who then returned it to us with everything inside. I learn a lot from my precious "Beatrice," who leads me out of the Dantesque Selva Oscura toward the vision of Paradise. She has helped before, guiding my hands to climb up the wall to teach new arm muscles to work. A radical mastectomy removes the pectoral muscles and the spare parts, and the upper arm muscles have to be trained to take over. What a splendor our body is!

Licia and Teresa, after second surgery, 1976

When our Licia was five years old, we took her to Italy for the first time. Our relatives were delighted, especially my uncle Bruno, my beloved Zia Maria's husband, who made lovely miniature furniture for Licia's dollhouse. Licia would stand beside him in his furniture shop, in awe at how he could create such beautiful works from a piece of wood.

In Reggio Calabria, we visited our uncle Ottavio, my father's youngest brother, his family and his five-year-old granddaughter, Emanuela. Uncle Ottavio decided to take us to the Greek Theater in Taormina, Sicily, an eventful voyage. As soon we sat on the ferry boat, Emanuela began her work as a guide, well versed in the mythology of the area. "Licia, look at the statue of Aeolus, the god of the wind, which drove Odysseus's boats off course from reaching Ithaca, where they were returning to. And now we are going to pass Scylla and Charybdis, the two sea monsters that destroyed most of Odysseus's fleets as they crossed the Straights of Messina." My poor Licia began to shiver and asked me if we were going to meet any more monsters or gods. I reassured her that we were safe, but then Emanuela called out to her saying: "When I see another god I will tell you more." Licia rolled her eyes, hoping there were no more gods. In Taormina, we visited the Greek Theater, Emanuela climbing the steps like she belonged there, I sitting on those stone steps beside her, and imagining the Greeks performing on the stage at sunset, facing the stage, outside with Mount Etna, the fuming volcano, as backdrop. What an enchantment!

Back in Reggio, my aunt Nella decided that Licia was too skinny, probably because she did not eat enough, an alarm for a southern Italian mother, whose main preoccupation is to prepare good food to plump up their children. Poor Licia. My aunt would follow her to the bathroom to make sure she really needed to be there and not as an avoidance of food. With Emanuela and her gods, which seemed to appear everywhere, my aunt's pressure to eat, and my uncle's pressure to have her buy more and bigger things, Licia was happiest when we decided to leave for Capistrano.

GRADUATIONS

Licia's high school graduation, 1988

As a present for Licia's high school graduation, I decided to take her to France, the mecca for Impressionist fans, where we visited the Musée d'Orsay in Paris. We spent days feasting our eyes on the Monet lilies, which covered whole walls, a sea of blue with delicate pink and white water lilies moving through calm waters, now alone, now in groups. Upstairs we delighted in the Post-Impressionists like Cézanne, considered the father of modern painting.

From Paris we took a train to Marseille and then a smaller one to Aix-en-Provence, where Cézanne's house and atelier sat on a graceful hill overlooking Mont Sainte-Victoire, which he painted repeatedly at different times of the day, as the mountain changed colors. Licia and I arrived at the house early in the afternoon, and to kill time we sat on a bench, overlooking a gate, where an old French lady was sitting and presumably also waiting. I introduced myself and sat beside her and began a long conversation in French. Teary-eyed, she told me that she came to say goodbye to this treasure before it was demolished to build apartments. I took her hand and comforted her, telling her that according to the local morning paper, an American journalist reported the sad news to the museums association in New York, and they immediately began negotiating to buy the building and give it to the University of Aix to manage.

The sweet old lady dried her eyes and gave me a beautiful smile and a great story. She told us that when she was a little girl, Cézanne would stop by her house on the way to Mont Sainte-Victoire to have coffee with her mother, stopping by again on his return home. She was very jealous of the attention her mother gave him, and one day when he offered her one of his paintings, she refused it. "Now I am saddened, of course, although I would have given it to the museum," she said. The museum opened and we left the dear old lady still sitting on the bench.

The house was the same as Cézanne left it. Most of the visitors were Americans and, not understanding the French guide, would ask for help from others near them. This annoyed the French guide, and giving the Americans a stern look, she made a derogatory remark. Not able to withstand her arrogance, I asked where she came from, and she brusquely responded that she was a student from the University at Aix-en-Provence. I asked her if she had read the local paper that morning and she said no. I asked her in French to permit me to tell her the biggest news of the day: the Americans had bought Cézanne's house and atelier and donated it to her university. And they bought it with the taxes and donations these people in her group paid, the very people she had denigrated. I told her she was not fit to lead this or any group. I told the Americans to look around and feel comfortable to talk and ask questions, for this was their museum. My Licia felt embarrassed, but I apologized to her at a wonderful supper in a restaurant on one of the side streets of this little jewel.

The next morning we took a bus to Arles to visit Vincent van Gogh's home, where he and Paul Gauguin lived for a while before Vincent went crazy and cut his own ear off. The room was exactly as it was in the painting. Then we went to see the place where he had lived with Dr. Gachet and painted the beautiful nearby wheat fields. It was a wonderful trip, which we had to cut short because Licia was not feeling well. We returned to Aix, where unfortunately, I was robbed in a beautiful cathedral I was visiting and appeared to be deserted. The skillful thief opened my purse without my realizing it and took my Canadian passport and wallet. I reported it immediately to the police, but they just laughed, saying that there are many thieves circulating the city. My Licia commented that the Neapolitans might have a bad reputation, but they were no worse than the French. I informed the Canadian Consulate in Italy, our next destination, but with my Italian passport we had no problem there.

We met my cousin Gigi in Cremona, where we visited the violin makers and particularly one, Bissolotti, who was the best known. Mr. Bissolotti invited us to his house and atelier and showed us some of the many violins he had made. Licia played some of them but was fixed on an old violin, and did not want to buy one from Mr. Bissolotti, a big mistake as it turned out, for his violins are now unaffordable. From there we went to the museum to see the Stradivari, Guarneri and Amati violins and to hear the master of the museum play them, which he did every day. What a treat; Gigi was beside himself, for he aspired to become a violin maker. The next day we boarded the plane for Detroit, where we had a long wait at the immigration office because I only had my Italian passport. They finally let us go, and when we met Thomas they asked Judge Carlson why he didn't tell them right away I was his wife. He shook their hands and we left.

Licia and Teresa, concert at Vassar

Licia's graduation at Vassar for her BA was a great event; she played a violin concerto with a piano accompanist for her thesis in music performance. She had a second major in philosophy. What a joyous occasion. Thomas's parents drove all the way to Poughkeepsie from Muskegon, Michigan, to see their Licia graduate, even though they were in their eighties. Some friends from the International School also came, Mrs. Mardigan with her son Joshua, and

Justin Steger, two of my favorite boys, who brought Licia flowers after the performance. We had a beautiful reception afterward in one of the beautiful halls on campus. For me it was more than a concert and graduation; it was a survival from cancer and being able to see my little Licia grown into a beautiful, intelligent and kind lady.

Hilary, Carmen and Licia, Vassar concert reception

Teresa, Licia and Tom, Vassar concert reception

After Vassar our Licia went to the University of Toronto to pursue a master's and PhD in philosophy, and she had many occasions to visit with my mother, who lived not too far from the university.

Mother Renda and Licia, University of Toronto

She experienced my mother's cooking and learned to eat many foods, like *verdure*, a typical dish in her cuisine. Licia would take my mother to doctors and experienced many funny and embarrassing moments. Once, when they went to the ophthalmologist after her cataract surgery, a black patch still on her right eye, upon entering the room she remarked: "Licia qui' siamo tutti pirati" (Licia, here we are all pirates). When it was her turn to see the doctor to test her eyesight for a pair of glasses, Licia translated: "Nonna, quali vedi meglio, 1 o 2" (Nonna, which number do you see better, 1 or 2). She responded: "Io non lo so, andiamo, che questo non capisce niente" (I don't know! He's the doctor. Let's go, he doesn't know anything).

Once a week Licia would meet my mother at Bar Italia

for lunch, and one of these times Licia arrived late. She asked people outside if they had seen an old lady pass by, but they all said they had not, and that they were all probably home eating. After a while she decided to check inside and there was Nonna, seated, with her dark sunglasses and short skirt, having already ordered. She scolded Licia for always being late. My poor Licia, with Nonna no one wins.

Her graduation from University of Toronto was another wonderful event. The Carlsons came and stayed with us at a beautiful hotel on Avenue Road, decorated in the English style, which Mother Carlson loved. After the PhD ceremony, we all went to a lovely restaurant and then for dessert at my sister Gina's house. What a treat to be all together. Our Licia gave and continues to give us many joys.

Tom, Mother Carlson, Licia and Father Carlson, PhD graduation

Gina, Licia, Mother & Father Carlson, and torta made by Gina, PhD reception

Another chapter in Licia's life began when she moved to New York City, a city she loved very much. She worked at the *New York Times*, in the international section, answering complaints and questions from all over the world. She loved it and lived the daily life of a New Yorker, always in movement. After the *New York Times*, she taught a few classes at John Jay College of Criminal Justice while waiting for a full-time position in a university philosophy department. She applied to many and went to interviews as far away as Seattle. She got the job at Seattle University, where she remained for a long time.

After a few months in Seattle, Licia learned that Jeremiah Frank, a Vassar friend, was also in Seattle, doing his specialty training in family practice at Washington University Medical School. They got together, and their friendship developed into an engagement and wedding in Seattle, a city they both loved very much. They were especially enthralled by Mount Rainier, which loomed in the background, changing with the light, not unlike Mont Sainte-Victoire in Aix-en-Provence. Licia was so in love with Mount Rainier that on our first trip to Seattle, she made sure she got us seats near the window on the side of the plane that presented the best and spectacular view. How thoughtful our Licia was.

Jeremiah and Licia, wedding, 2003

Thomas and I both liked Seattle very much, and we came for a number of concerts Licia played with the Seattle Symphony Orchestra and the chamber music ensemble of which she was a part. On the way home from one of the concerts, we took a bus full of drunkards. I became concerned for Licia taking this bus alone after concerts, and I convinced Thomas that she needed a car, which we purchased soon after. We met Jeremiah, whom we liked very much, and we agreed that he was the perfect man for Licia; caring, intelligent and gentle.

The wedding was to be held on the top floor of a beautiful hotel with a splendid view of Seattle and the mountain. They planned the wedding, at which Thomas officiated and a rabbi represented the Jewish heritage. Jeremiah's parents gave beautiful readings, and I sang the "Ave Maria," accompanied by Licia's chamber music ensemble. The nuptial program's cover had a memorable quote from Kahlil Gibran, which was read during the ceremony by friends Lara, Corinne and Matthew.

> And in the sweetness of friendship
> Let there be laughter, and
> sharing of pleasures.
> For in the dew of little things the
> heart finds its morning
> And is refreshed.

Licia's friends Carola and Kristen read from *Letters to a Young Poet*, by Rainer Maria Rilke; Licia's friend Katherine's young boys, Beno and Elias, who were very dear to Licia, read selections on love; Yvonne and Deborah, friends of

Jeremiah's, read "The Sunflowers" by Mary Oliver, a poetess whom Jeremiah admired; and the readings ended with the parental blessings from Margaret and Murray Frank, followed by the "Ave Maria," sung by yours truly. The vows and the exchange of rings ended the ceremony, followed by a reception and a sumptuous meal, "surf and turf" or fish as entrees. Licia had gone to the famous Pike Place Market that morning and bought sunflowers and blue irises, magnificently arranged as centerpieces. After dinner, while the chamber orchestra was playing, Licia and Jeremiah distributed the *bomboniere* (little favors) which my friends and I had assembled in Detroit.

Jeremiah and Licia with the *bomboniere*

Most of our friends came: Ellen and Denis, Mary and Clyde, Linda and Henry, Licia's best friend, Tania, Hillary and her girls Melanie and Brittany, Carmen, Thomas's brother Bruce, and many other friends of Licia's and Jeremiah's.

Jeremiah, Licia and friends, wedding, 2003

We also met Jeremiah's family for the first time: his father Murray and his wife Joanna, his mother Peggy, his brother Nathanial, half brother Peter, half sister Lisa and her family, all wonderful people who became very dear to us.

Murray and Licia, Toronto, 2003

The day before the wedding, Licia's friends Kirsten, Carola and Jenny thought it would be a nice idea to have a trousseau party to show the beautiful work by my sisters and mother. There I met Jeremiah's aunt Joan and her family, great people, very loving and kind.

My dearest niece Angela was the maid of honor, an effort of love for her and her family to come, given that two years earlier, their beloved Rita passed away, a death that shocked all of us. Angela was very brave and loved our Licia so much that she wanted to be there for her.

Licia and Angela, wedding reception, 2003

Because my family could not attend, given the distance, we decided to have a reception later in Toronto, at Bar Italia, which a lot of my friends also attended. What a memorable party, my mother there, waving her hand and saying "Hi, hi," for she did not want to kiss or shake hands.

THE MANY FACES OF WOMEN

Marianna, Mother Renda, Licia and Jeremiah, Toronto reception, 2003

Licia and Teresa, Toronto reception, 2003

Jeremiah and Licia moved to Boston, where he was born and raised, and we were happy for it was closer to us in Michigan. Licia began teaching at Harvard, where she remained for five years, and then got a job in the Philosophy Department at Providence College, in Rhode Island, where she is a full professor and still teaching.

In 2005 our Julian was born, and I managed to get the last flight for Boston, arriving just in time, in the middle of the night. After a long and difficult labor, with some tense moments, our Julian was born and I held him in my arms for the first time. What a joy! I was now a grandmother, one of the greatest gifts I have ever received.

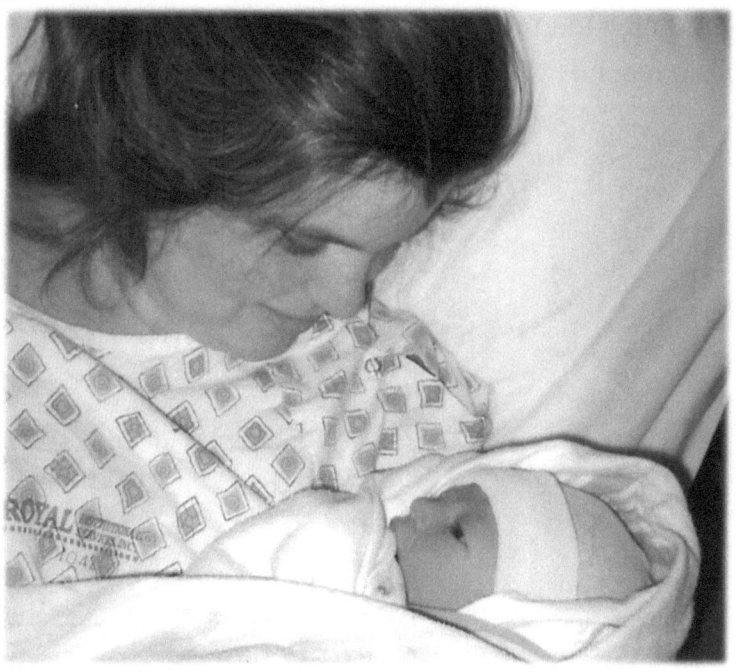

Licia and Julian, 2005

I stayed for a few days and then went home to relieve Thomas from watching my mother, who had come to live with us. Thomas was also anxious to hold this wondrous baby, and three months later the little family came to Detroit to present Julian to his great-grandparents. My mother exulted for joy in having another little boy in her family; then we went to Muskegon and Mother Carlson and Dad were equally jubilant, their first and only great-grandchild.

After our parents passed away, and my health began deteriorating, we decided to move to Boston in 2010 to be close to our family and be lucky enough to see our Julian grow up, a decision we never regretted. We were once again reunited with our Licia and her wonderful family.

Licia, Julian and Jeremiah

Julian, Teresa and Tom, Teresa becomes a U.S. citizen

Julian grew into a beautiful, intelligent young man who loves many things, one of which is writing poetry. One Christmas morning, our Julian surprised me. I found a beautiful paper rolled and tied with a red ribbon to the green branch of a tree, which I immediately opened, and here it is:

Stellina

Wisps of gray hair,
Papery skin

Barely brushing the flowery shawl draped over her shoulders.
Bright cherry lips, spread in a wide grin.
Revealing pearl white teeth, never touched by a cavity.

She exits the bathroom,
Ready to welcome the guests.
Arms wide open,
Mouthwatering smells wafting from the kitchen.

A true Italian grandmother,
Providing food, love, and support to her family.
Cooking is not a burden,
But an honor.

During the day, she tirelessly works in the garden,
At night, up in the study,
Writing her memoir,
Mozart in the background.

Selfless and brave,
Willing to do anything to help our family,
Supporting me
And encouraging me to do my very best.
Born in Italy, a small village in the south,
Capistrano.
She grew up playing with homemade toys,
Crafted from clay.

Clothes washed in the nearby brook,
The family farm yields a plentiful harvest.

REFLECTIONS FROM MY DIARY

Everything was homemade,
Dainty fingers sewing the only clothes they ever knew.

A long trek up the mountains, just for water.
Every year, looking forward to the grape harvest.

Her whole childhood spent in beautiful Italy,
Lush green pastures,
Mountains touching the sky.
Beaches spread as far as the eye can see,
Reaching for the horizon.

And little Capistrano nestled in the middle,
So small, there was only one tiny shop.
Everyone was family,
They were all welcome.

She braved through one of the most dangerous times,
A child during the Second World War,
Born under a bridge,
Bombs falling,
Nazis crawling through the mountains like ants on an ant hill,
And a newborn baby,
Hungry,
Sobbing,
Scared.

To prevent exposure, her grandfather was almost forced to kill her,
But a loving aunt took her in,
Protecting her for the first few years.

Through the remainder of the war she lived,
Her family hiding,
Praying for the war to end,
And every now and then accepting some chocolate
From the American soldiers.

She survived,
Thrived,
And even gave poop to a Nazi.

At seventeen her voyage began,
And on the Vulcania she sailed.
Two nauseating weeks,
Alone with Mom,
Headed off to a new world with new opportunity.

In Toronto, she went to high school.
The new Italian girl, without a word of English.
Her degree was acquired in university,
And she taught for a number of years.

Then it was off to the World's Fair
And amongst the music and crowds,
She met Thomas,
My sweet and loving grandfather.

Thirty-eight years later, I came,
And somewhere in those years, she had
Cancer, not once but three times,
Two heart attacks,
One valve transplant,
And a whole lot of complications.

I heard her story,
And I was inspired by my grandmother.

She is a survivor.
Never giving up hope,
Always looking at the bright side,
Even when the horizon is dark.

And I can only hope that someday,
I will be like her.

Julian 2018

My Julian is very much like his parents, a healer, as I experienced many times, especially during a long journey with an ulcerated foot. He would come and hold my hand and tell me to breathe in and out when his father changed the bandage. Then, as a reward for my being brave, Julian would play his cello, or stay with me when the rest of the household went to Licia's concerts. He would play music, tell me stories and occasionally prepare a wonderful risotto for us. What a treasure we have.

MY BOTTICELLI

One morning I received a beautiful letter from my Botticelli, my Noelle, one of the students in the International School, which I directed for many years and where I got to know many inspiring parents and students from many countries. But among all of them, Noelle captured my attention, when she was in preschool, for her artistic way of dressing and fixing her voluminous, curly blond hair, the color of wheat, which cascaded on her shoulders and framed her beautiful face. I saw in front of me a miniature Botticelli, the "Birth of Venus" or "La Primavera." I knew that we had an artist among us, and it helped that her mother taught art at the school.

I followed Noelle through the years and we became very close. She wrote and directed a play for her graduation from Northwestern, and even though I was recovering from cancer I went by train to be with her. We spent the whole day in her room, reading Rilke to calm her and discussing how she should let her actors and actresses speak, uninhibited by their director. In the evening we met her parents and had a lovely dinner afterward.

Noelle still visits me and we share our writings, our thoughts and our angsts. I love our visits both in the U.S. and abroad, where I visited her and her family in Germany. I love being with Noelle and anxiously wait for the end of the pandemic so we can resume our visits. I need my Botticelli to inspire and heal me. This is the latest letter she sent me.

Dearest Teresa,

How are you? How is your health and your foot? Thinking of you much and sending much love and healing. Things are good here in NY, some ups and downs, and continuing to engage with my health situation (with my hip and leg), but healing slowly. I have learned so much from you about healing... and I always think of your courage, patience, strength and ability to open into deeper lessons of life through the challenges. I feel that I am deep in the winter months—and taking time to be inward and restful, with my body and heart—and am grateful for this time of restful transformation.

I finished your first book on Sunday evening. It was

so beautiful, and transported me in all the ways. I was with you in your village, by your side, listening to you share your stories and feelings with the river. I could feel the bark on the olive trees, the smell of its oil and the playfulness of the children. I watched the rituals and prayers and processions and felt the weight and grief of the war. Your words took me on a powerful journey into the infinite and the daily life of your childhood.

And I just wanted to offer immense gratitude to you... for everything really. The book, your stories, your village, your connection with nature, how you have taken the greatest internal journeys and found connection with the epic stories and songs of operas. I want to offer gratitude to you for the International School of my childhood—for the environment you created, your vision, and all the seeds you watered in me—seeds of creativity and vision, of nature and ritual, of performance and community. Of honoring the creative and magical spirit of children above all else, children from countries all over, that span the globe.

When I read your book, I saw so much of myself in it. It wasn't like I had lived that same experience, so it wasn't a mirror—but more that I saw how much of your childhood, of your experiences, you allowed to move through you and lived them. *This* is reflected in the lessons you have taught me, the space you created for me to live my truth—with and through art and nature and spirit—and how I am able to pass this on to the youth I work with now.

You have always been a friend, a collaborator, a mentor, a mother, a teacher, a sister and connected spirit on this journey of life.

I hold your stories deep in my heart, and I look forward to reading the next *Oddyssey* books in time.

Celebrating you today and always,

Your Botticelli,

Noelle xxx

Noelle in Teresa's garden in Detroit

I met many other wonderful students at the International School, some of whom have gone on to great success. Sam is with the U.S. State Department, and his sister Abby is an excellent teacher in a tough school system in California. Justin, Melanie and Brittany are doing great things: our Melanie went to South Africa to teach miners how to manage their finances; Justin was the darling of the school, very interested in cinematography; and Brittany, his charming sister, is developing into a lovely young lady. Cielle and Lucas are very successful in their professions, and the Karoukis boys are in the medical profession. Joshua and Nathan bought an olive orchard in California and produce the best oil, which I love and order often. The name is NOVO and I taste my oil from Capistrano in their olive groves.

There is Sarah Reed, my other goddess, who resembled one of two girls in a portrait hanging in the Detroit Institute of Arts. Every time I went I visited the room where the portrait was hanging and recalled those deep blue eyes, the color of the Mediterranean Sea. Sarah's cascading blond hair fell onto her shoulders like the hair of our Madonna of the Mountains in Capistrano. Still other students come to mind: Amir, his brother and their sister Michelle; Lea, Misha and Brandy; Sasha and Sally. Sasha is the only student I know who got an MA from Harvard, and his sister, Sally, the only one able to follow the program with the French students, got her law degree.

There were the Mansouri children, Natasha, the beauty with emerald green eyes, and Nicolai, the little prince; the Italian children like Camilla and Judita; and many others. Mr. and Mrs. Kast helped the school very much and had two sons enrolled. Alex, the younger, was a great artist; he painted a crucifix in the style of the 1500s, a real masterpiece, which he gave to me and which I still treasure in my home. Lucas was very intelligent, conscious of time and did not appreciate when it was wasted by teachers who indulged in telling their personal stories. For example, the guitar teacher after school talked too much, according to Lucas, who had come to my office to discuss the problem. Lucas subsequently told the teacher that Mrs. Carlson did not appreciate him wasting Lucas's time, for he was a serious student.

I think I need to write another book to include them all, my wonderful students who inspired and taught me a great deal about life, how to be a good listener, and a life learner.

10

Reunited

We expand, we grow, and like stars we contract into old age, the dark age, the black hole, which leads us to total absorption into ourselves and the universe, where there is no differentiation between matter and spirit. My mother is a concrete example of this theory of mine.

At age 62 I had a baby. I did not plan to have her, yet I should have known sooner or later she would come to me. I did not plan to have her, for at my age one is usually done with child rearing and embraces the world community with its many causes to partake in. I had the feeling that I was becoming part of the universal community, the community of humans. I enjoyed this new awareness. This was the result of many years of professional work, and the time available to open my house, my gardens and lunches to people of every race and creed, friends and acquaintances. My abode had expanded to include all, and in this inclusiveness I failed to notice that a greater demand was descending upon me, as imperceptibly and gently as the first signs of spring. I continued my active life, oblivious to all, with no preparation for the great challenge awaiting me. No preparation, no bathroom bars, no diapers, no idea of the night care needed. No preparation whatsoever, even though my mother was getting older, for she appeared indestructible, despite her age of 93 and her deep sorrow after the loss of her granddaughter Rita, and a year later, of her daughter (and my sister) Nina, who had taken care of her, as they lived in the same house.

I continued to follow the marvelous path of living, making every day an event, learning, growing in many ways, giving and receiving in my beautiful gardens, a marvel of beauty and harmony, a simplicity of form and colors, with stones perfectly raked every morning to express the theme of the day. My world was a perfect fusion of cultures, culinary indulgences and spiritual encounters, until the phone rang one day.

Mother had fallen while taking out the garbage and was now at the Toronto Western Hospital. I arrived there, and the first thing I saw were cafes with delicious smells of coffee, and an array of pastries with cinnamon and vanilla scents, enveloping me in an aura of peace and voluptuousness. Like Ulysses called by the Sirens to the water, I wanted to sit and enjoy one of those delights, but my conscience would not allow it. I took the elevator to the big room in the orthopedic department. I immediately knew my mother would not like being there, so I asked if she could be transferred to a private or semi-private room. They informed me that insurance would not cover it, so I opted to assume the expenses. She was happy; a room with two people, her bed near the window.

Seeing so many people with broken bones in the orthopedic department did not stop her from commenting: "Gesù, tutti cadimu a Toronto." ("Everyone falls in Toronto.") The nurses could not understand why she did not speak English after forty years of living in an English-speaking country. But, this is our Nonna! Her universe was shrinking and returning to her childhood. She needed a mother, a loving mother. Was I to become her mother? She was not a child but a grown lady who now needed all the care a child needs, yet she wanted to remain in control of her life. I didn't blame her for that. She was always in control of us children, and of her orphaned brothers and sisters before us when she was only ten.

Hospital time was for planning, to assess the care she would need after rehabilitation and where she would go. My sister Pina came from Montreal and wanted Mother to go and live with them. She would enjoy the farm, we told her, but she refused. She wanted to go back to her house and die there when the time came, she said. But the doctors would not discharge her unless someone lived with her. Our Angela wanted to take her, but Nonna found her house tumultuous; too many people coming and going. She would have loved to live with Gina and the five boys, whom she adored, but our Gina was sick with severe vasculitis and fell often herself.

I was the last resort, but if I could not do it with total dedication and love, I thought an assisted living facility would be better. But would she survive, not speaking English and surrounded by strangers, in an institution, in Toronto, in the U.S., even in Italy? My mother was a universal being, despite her monolingualism. After discussing the matter with my beloved Thomas, we decided to bring her to the U.S. She lived with us for three years, three years of joy for me, that I was finally reunited with my mother.

Mother Renda, Teresa, Tom and Licia, Detroit

She was a wonderful lady and enjoyed my friends, who would come to visit her and bring delicious food; especially "la signora del riso," my friend Fatimé, whose tahdig rice (scorched Persian rice) was her favorite. We celebrated her ninety-third birthday in our house, and she received the most beautiful bouquet of yellowish orange roses from my friend Mary Kelly. Then we went across the street to our neighbor's house for dessert. When we returned home my gracious female neighbor took her arm to help her, but she refused, saying the gentlemen will take me home. With a "gentleman" on each arm, we all proceeded like on a procession back to the house, with mother walking even better than before. She never lost her preference for men.

Fatimé invited us to her house for dinner one day and my mother accepted immediately. Dressed beautifully, and well perfumed, we had the wonderful tahdig, the crusty rice at the bottom of the rice pan. After dinner, dancing began, with mother happy as a lark, singing in her head. After a while I asked her if she was tired and wanted to go home, but she said what's the hurry, and we stayed until very late. She loved being there, for she admired Fatimé's organized and clean environment, full of beautiful things, and was most impressed by the bathroom full of mirrors that made the room seem endless.

For her ninety-fifth birthday, we celebrated at a restaurant in the neighborhood. Our friends Hilary, Mary and Carmen from the International School came.

Mother Renda, 95th birthday, Detroit

The restaurant was known for its great food, and Mother ordered veal with mashed potatoes and gravy, which covered the meat. She ate with such gusto that a big piece of veal got stuck in her throat. The restaurant is frequented by many doctors, and fortunately that evening there were quite a few. Two of them immediately came to help and laid her on the floor. My mother looked around and whispered "Madonna, com'e' sporco questo pavimento" ("Madonna, how dirty this floor is"). Unfortunately, there was no success in dislodging the meat, so we brought her to a nearby hospital by ambulance, where they did a little surgery and dislodged the meat, but advised her to stay overnight, which she did not like.

The next day she was told she would not be discharged until a speech therapist came to see her. It was close to noon and Nonna knew that if she went home in the afternoon she would be charged for a full day's stay. Finally a young, delicate blond lady came in and tried to examine Nonna, upon which Nonna grabbed her neck with such a strong grip that we had to call security to dislodge her. Needless to say, Nonna was immediately discharged—before noon.

Because of Nonna's age, a young doctor and his nurse would come visit her once a month. But the doctor would show up at noon, a sacrosanct time for her, and she did not want any intrusions during her lunchtime. One time I was making pizza for lunch, and as customary, the doctor showed up. I invited them to have pizza with us and they accepted. We had a drink, and the doctor made a toast to Mother that she would be around to celebrate her 100th birthday. "Spovianto, non io" ("God forbid, not I"). A few months later she died in her bed, peacefully, and we brought her body to Toronto, to be interred near my father.

Our Nonna is gone now; no more beautiful smiles and singing in the morning as she sips her coffee in bed. I shall miss that smile, that Leonardoesque smile, veiled, but piercing my soul. Despite the difficulty of the daily tasks, she was a companion for me, an anchor, a sea of tranquility, and a field of peace in a world of travail. Her presence, her countenance, her simplicity, her wisdom, all spoke of other worlds, much more human, her village. Her departure left a void in my heart, which echoed throughout the house. We were like two rivers that had come together after a long separation, only to be separated again as she joined the Greater Sea.

At the funeral in Toronto I had to eulogize my

beautiful mother. I opened with some words from Padre Pio: "Peace is the simplicity of the spirit, the serenity of the mind, the tranquility of the soul, the hope of love" (translated from the Italian).

Love, my mother had in abundance. She loved her daughters, her family, and her husband, as well as her neighbors, which comprised the whole village, and, above all, she loved herself. In loving herself she taught all of us how to survive the vicissitudes of life. My mother spoke little but when she opened her mouth, wise words poured out as easily as the waters of our beloved fountain in the piazza. She remains for us still a source of comfort and inspiration, for her many utterances of wisdom will live on as long as we live.

A poem I wrote for the shocking death of our Rita remained in my diary, unable to be read, until now, after the passing of my mother:

> Comforting, comforted...
> Giving, receiving
> A caressing hand, a hug, tears
> Streaming down every face
> Silently, emanating from the hearts
> Broken by the thunder of the day.
>
> Every gesture spoke of love,
> Inextinguishable by the darkness of the day.

The candle on the white table witnessed it all
And tried to burn assiduously
Uncoerced by it all, burning faintly but solemnly;

Keeping pace with the tears
Which flowed gently but steadily
From the river of the heart.

Every movement,
Slow and gentle
Spoke of the deep sorrow
Of life, of death, of giving and of taking...
A sorrow that enveloped all of us
With a mantle of profound SILENCE,
The silence of the cloistered monastery
Interrupted by prayers and Gregorian chants.
Words ceased to have power.

Like the painting of Millet, *The Angelus*,
Everyone stood still and listened to the bells within
Speaking of loss, of love, of endurance,
Call to contemplation, to meditation, to quietude...

The children too, heard the Angelus,
Gently smiling, quietly roaming around the room
In reverence of the pain
That enveloped us all.

Post Scriptum

TRE DONNE DI CAPISTRANO (in italiano per le loro famiglie)

NONNA TERESA

Nonna Teresa è la mamma di Rosanna Natale, e ha vissuto sempre con la figlia crescendole i tre adorabili figli, Francesco, Daniele e Marco i quali nutrono per la nonna un amore profondo; a volte si litigano chi dorme con la nonna costringendola a fare loro il turno. In una delle mie visite, mio cugino Luigi, il papà dei ragazzi insistette che io rimanessi con loro durante il mio soggiorno a Capistrano and in uno dei pomeriggi dopo un sontuoso pranzo facemmo il consueto pisolino. Io non potendo dormire, mi alzai per leggere il giornale, vado in cucina e vedo Francesco seduto vicino la nonna che leggeva un brano dalle opere di Ovid, il poeta latino. Io interrompo

Francesco e gli chiedo perché legge in Latino, una lingua ignota alla nonna. Egli mi risponde "Zia, non importa se la nonna capisca o no, ella adora ascoltare il suono della mia voce." Rimasi stupita ma impressionata dall'amore profondo tra nonna e nipoti imprimendo nella mia psiche questa vignetta di gesti memorabili.

Nonna Teresa è una donnina di statura media ma di un sorriso così coinvolgente che ognuno di noi che varca quella soglia rimane incantata. Essa prepara cibi squisiti per tutti e a volte ci onora con il suo piatto speciale: Pipi e Patate, cotte alla perfezione emanando un profumo che la gente che passa davanti casa grida: "Teresa, cosa state preparando che manda questo piacevole odore." Era ed è il mio piatto preferito. Daniele, ora un uomo che lavora a Serra San Bruno ritorna a casa ogni giorno a pranzo verso l'una e dopo un pisolino ritorna al lavoro. Aspetta a cuocere la pasta finche non sono tutti e tre a casa, anche se qualcuno chiede di mangiare subito, ella con quel sorriso e voce calma dice loro d'aspettare con pazienza. Che rispetto da' ad ognuno, che lezioni di vita insegna loro.

Quando Nonna Teresa doveva essere operata, Luigi e Rosanna l'accompagnarono a Milano nella migliore clinica; Rosanna impegnata con la scuola ritornò a casa e Luigi rimase con lei per lungo tempo Durante una visita all'ospedale, una signora là con il suo ammalato, chiese a Luigi se la Signora Teresa era sua madre, ma rimase stupita quando Luigi le disse che essa era sua suocera. Il nostro

Luigi è stato sempre e rimane una persona eccezionale pieno di bontà e magnanimo con tutti.

Nonna Teresa è molto amata da tutti a Capistrano specialmente dai suoi nipoti che stravedono per lei. Durante un suo collasso cardiaco durante la notte, Francesco, il più grande dei tre, se la mette in macchina e la porta all'ospedale di Vibo Valentia, guidando nel buio in quelle strade ripide, strette con un'infinità di curve attorniate di sentieri con piante che rendono il tutto in una visione macabra. Anche io feci quel percorso di notte e sento ancora i brividi nel rievocarlo. Ma il nostro coraggioso Francesco non ebbe timore, la sua preoccupazione era della nonna e le parlava continuamente per far sì che essa non si abbandonasse al collasso. Arrivati all'ospedale, dopo una intensa visita informarono Francesco che la doveva portare subito a Catanzaro, un'altra città, circa cento kilometri di distanzadove l'avrebbero operata al cuore. L'ospedale di Vibo si mise subito in contatto con quello di Catanzaro e la nonna sopravvisse il tutto. Che donna forte, voleva vivere per vedere il suo Francesco sposarsi.

Ho sempre ammirato questa donna dolce come lo zucchero, accogliente con tutti, una cuoca par eccellenza, forte come una pianta d'olivo, sempre sorridente e paziente. Mi ha insegnato molto e ringrazio il Signore che l'ho conosciuta.

THE MANY FACES OF WOMEN

Nonna Teresa

POST SCRIPTUM

LA MIA SALVATRICE, ZIA MARIA

Dopo la morte della sua mamma, zia Maria perse l'appetito di vivere con un padre arrogante ed autoritario. Ma dove andare? Decise di entrare nel convento delle Carmelite dove le sorelle Natali di Capistrano erano già diventate monache. Che perdita per la mia mamma, due sorelle via da casa, senza mamma e molti fratelli ed un padre indomabile, che accudiva giornalmente. Durante la seconda guerra nel 1942, la zia rientra a Capistrano e trova la casa vuota. Erano tutti accampati sotto il ponte vicino all'olificio, aspettando la mia nascita che avvenne al buio, sotto la luce della candela. Subito la bimba si mise a strillare, aveva freddo e fame nonostante i tentativi della mamma ad allattarla, non aveva latte, la paura delle bombe le aveva fatto perdere il latte. Al pianto assordante il nonno pose la sua mano gigante sulla bocca della bambina per farla zittire. Zia Maria capì all'istante che qualcosa malefica stava succedendo, si lancia verso il nonno e gli morde la mano, prende la creatura, l'avvolge in una bandiera italiana che aveva con se, e si diede alla fuga nel pieno della notte.

Dopo un bel pó di corsa, si fermò vicino al fiume, lo stesso fiume che alimentava l'olificio. Esausta si addormenta tenendo la bimba avvolta nel mantello di monaca. All'alba si svegliaal canto degli uccelli, guarda verso il suo seno e vede la bimba che poppava. Si mise ad intonare le preghiere mattutine tra le quali l'Ave Maria soffermandosi sulle parole: Benedetta fra le donne... Anche io sono benedetta fra le donne, oggi mi è accaduto un miracolo, il miracolo di essere mamma... Che miracolo! Intona con giubilo "anche se non sei venuta dal mio ventre, oggi sei mia." Anche dopo che ebbe i suoi figli, mi considerava la sua prima figlia. Ho sempre adorato questa donna, anche se per diciassette anni nessuno inclusa lei, parlò della mia nascita. Quante volte glielo chiesi alla mia famiglia, alle vecchie sedute sulle soglie delle case discutendo di tutto, ma mai della mia nascita.

Giorni prima della mia partenza per il Canada, andammo a Serra San Bruno per visitare il monastero. Là sulla grande scalinata ci sedemmo e lei mi raccontò l'evento della mia nascita, che racconto in *Oddyssey*, libro uno. Alla fine del racconto, si alzò come Medea in teatro e mi offerse la bimba dicendo: "Prendila, è una vita che la cerchi." Presi la bimba e me la strinsi al cuore, mi sentii rinascere, finalmente mi sono ritrovata prima della mia partenza, al Monastero rifugio dalle bombe della guerra. Quanti ricordi della mia zia erano chiusi nella valigetta di cartone che portammo con noi in Canada. Il viaggio è stato lungo e pericoloso nonché pauroso, l'immagine Leonardesca della mia zia mi diede forza, coraggio e speranza di ritornare da lei un giorno. Infatti ci ritornai nel mille novecento sessanta sette e la trovai in forma, vibrante con una forza invidiabile, con amore profondo verso i suoi figli e Chiazzarello, il suo fondo dove donna e natura s'incontravano per celebrare la vita. Chiazzarello era un luogo di lavoro, di benessere creato dalle sue mani; un luogo di preghiera dove lei s'incontrava con l'Eterno intonando inni di gioia e di ringraziamento. Una mamma per me, un'insegnante di vita con le sue gesta ed i suoi atti. E stata la mia confortatrice, quando mi sentivo giù che mi capitava spesso, andavo da lei per svuotarmi l'animo. Le raccontavo le mie anzietà, le mie nuove angosce che si manifestavano a galoppo quasi ogni giorno. Lei mi calmava, dandomi un fico secco, mi si sedeva vicina e mi raccontava delle storie, una delle quali mi ha molto impressionata che la ricordo ancora e sento il bisogno di comunicarvela.

C'era una volta un baco da seta che ha deciso di mangiare poco per non chiudersi in un bozzolo e diventare un baco da seta. Una notte mentre tutti dormivano, decise di lasciare il suo milieu, la cucina dove viveva con moltissimi altri bachi che mangiavano senza posa finche si chiudevano nel bozzolo, il loro sepolcro. Un buco nella finestra gli offerse l'uscita. Per primo si sentì gioiosa di essere in un grande luogo alberato, pieno di fiori sotto una grande cupola blue con nuvole che si muovevano spontaneamente. Amava la pioggia che le cascava addosso, rendendo la sua pelle luccicante come le stelle, ed il sole con il suo calore rinvigorante l'asciugava. Non aveva mai visto un tale mondo, la sola cosa che lei conosceva era di essere un uovo, che il calore la trasformava in larva che mangiava a morte. Si sentiva fortunata di essere in queste meraviglie, ma nello stesso tempo si sentiva sola in queso mondo dove sapeva di non appartenervi; era triste quando vedeva gli uccelli volare in flocchi, le farfalle saltellando insieme posandosi sulle corolle dei fiori. Egli non aveva nessuno con cui condividere tali meraviglie, la sua specie aveva scelto di seguire la propria tradizione, la tradizione di mangiare a non finire e poi morire.

Mentre stava scivolando di qua e di là uno di questi giorni, alzò la sua testolina e vide una signora stendere al sole nel suo balcone delle tele di seta di colori vari ed abbaglianti che la colpir ono profondamente. Cammin facendo ne vide mole altre sventolare al vento dai vari balconi uguali ad altre tante tele. Potevano forse essere tessute col filo dei moltissimi bozzi che giacevano con lei sulle enormi ceste che rosolavano senza posa le foglie del gelso? Pensò a lungo e divenne triste al pensiero che pure lei poteva essere una di quelle meravigliose tele. Lei aveva scelto d'abbandonare il suo dovere di baco da seta, di negare anni ed anni di tradizione a qual fine? La libertà, assaporarla; viverla nella solitudine, non appartenere a nessuno; ma la libertà'richiede responsabilità', si' vivere in solitudine, una straniera in un mondo dove bisogna appartenervi per sopravviverlo: accettare le meraviglie della natura prima ignota a lei; una natura di varietà e di bellezze incomparabili. La libertà richiede di accettare il bello ed il brutto.

Sono lieta d'avere ascoltato questa storia che ho scritto

anche in Inglese perché il messaggio è universale; LA VITA DEGLI EMIGRATI che lasciano il loro bozzolo, le loro terre per un mondo migliore che offre più possibilità di migliorare il loro destino. Si' hanno migliorato le loro possibilità economiche, ma hanno sofferto e soffrono tutt'oggi solitudine, discriminazioni, ed abusi, benché la non appartenenza—gravi prezzi da pagare. Fuggire dal proprio destino è un' impresa monumentale piena di duri fardelli e rammarici che ci perseguitano per sempre. "Chi lascia la via vecchia per la nuova, sa quel che lascia ma non quel che trova", un proverbio sulle labbra di ogni emigrante. (He who leaves the old road for the new one, knows what he leaves behind but not what he finds.)

Dopo aver finito di scrivere la storia del baco da seta raccontatemela dalla mia musa, mi chiesi perché questa tra molte, mi rimase incisa nella mia memoria e ne tirai fuori alcune osservazioni. Può essere che mia Zia tira fuori dal suo subconscio il fatto che sarei partita per l'America? E può essere che quel baco che fugge dal suo destino sia io? Forse questo baco da seta è ognuno di noi emigrati che vive tra sospiri ed accettazione: sospiri ogni qual volta la memoria si punta sul luogo natio, accettazione del nuovo mondo che offre anche momenti di gioia. La vita è una strada che ognuno di noi deve percorrere, una strada che eventualmente ci conduce alla conoscenza di noi stessi, del nostro animo, del nostro essere.

Zia Maria era la mia ancora dove mi appoggiavo nei

momenti di tristezza e di angosce che non erano pochi e mi svuotavo l'animo. Le raccontai la mia sofferenza per il baco da seta, che si chiudeva nel suo sepolcro vivo e là vi rimaneva immobile alla vita non aver conosciuto il mio fiume che mormorava la sua eterna canzone, l'aria che avvolgeva la terra, un manto azzurro dove sorvolavano nuvolette bianche o grigie ed un'imensità di alberi, fiori e deliziosi frutti. Mi ascoltava con pazienza ed amore dandomi il tempo necessario, poi mi dava un fico secco e m'invitava a sedermi vicina a lei tirando fuori dalla sua immensa caverna la storia che si addiceva al momento.

LA MIA ZIA ALBINA

Sembrava una bambolina, di statura media, un viso rotondo come la luna piena, sempre sorridente come il sole, calorosa ed una grande lavoratrice, un'affinità con la terra e la natura. La dea dell'agricoltura, sempre in movimento, ora seminava, annaffiava, coltivava qualsiasi tipo di grano, granturco, raccoglieva le olive, la maggior parte delle quali venivano trasformate in olio, le altre preparate in diversi modi, interi, schiacciati. Io adoravo vederla stendere i pomodorisu delle ceste enormi per farli seccare sotto il sole cocente. Poi preparava la salsa di pomodori, una tradizione Calabrese che si svolgeva in Autunno, la stagione più impegnativa per la mia Zia. Portava la merce dalla campagna in enormi ceste sulla testa mantenendo un'equilibrio come una ballerina. Quante cose hoimparato da lei, che tutt'oggi faccio anche io in un'altro continente, sotto un cielo diverso ma con le stesse procedure.

La festa di San Rocco era la mia preferita a casa di zia Albina: una enorme madia piena di dozzine e dozzine di uova fresche dalle sue galline che le giravano intorno intonando le loro melodie di soddisfazione di essersi liberate dal peso delle uova nel loro ventre. Io ero sempre presente per questo evento sacro e profano. Mi sembrava di essere in un laboratorio dove arti di ogni misura venivano modellati dalla pasta dolce dalle sue abili mani. Era una vera artista creando teste, corpi, parti del corpo conla precisione di uno scultore. La parte che mi faceva venire l'acquattino in bocca era verso la fine quando i voti usciti dal forno emanavano un profumo di vaniglia, poi zucchero sbattuto nel bianco delle uova finchè diventava una montagna bianca, che veniva spalmato con pennelli sugli arti. Noi bambini aspettavamo che le donne finissero di dipingere e poi dandoci il permesso di leccare le varie scodelle. Che piacere, mi sembrava di essere in cielo. La domenica di San Rocco le donne con le ceste piene di voti li offrivano al Santo sperando che Egli li guarisse dai loro mali. Il tutto veniva venduto all'asta. Mia madre che soffriva dal mal di testa offriva ilsuo voto che poi comprava assieme ad altri e li mangiavamo dopo il pranzo festivo. Zia Albina, donna di molti talenti nonostante un'infanzia dolorosa: perde la sua mamma a quattro anni e poi viene adottata dalla sorella del nonno che vive a Capistrano non lontano dalla casa materna. Soffrì molto lontana dalle sue sorelle e fratelli, specialmente il piccolo Totò che muore a due anni. Si abbandonò alla natura, che divenne la sua compagna e consolatrice.

La mia zia Albina, così chiamata perché è nata all'alba, una vera dea dell'alba, salutandola ogni mattina quando si alzava per incominciare la sua lunga giornata di lavoro nei campi o preparando il cibo per i contadini che lavoravano nella sue vasteproprietà, piantando, zappando, rastrellando, o assistere alla mietitura o trebbiatura del grano, nonché la vendemmia e la raccolta delle olive. C'era sempre lavoro per quelli che volevano guadagnarsi un pezzo di pane. Io adoravo specialmente la raccolta del grano, ammirando quegli uomini che sotto il sole cocente di luglio falciavano con delle falci enormi le piante di granole cui spighe ondeggiavano sotto il venticello creando un quadro in moto. Io guardavo e sognavo di essere una di quelle spighe, che poi diventavano il pane quotidiano, o uno di quegli uccelli che sorvolavano sopra i campi in cerca dei chicchi di grano. Molti di noi diventammo le spigolatrici raccogliendo le spighe rimaste per terra rischiando che un corvo si annidasse nei nostri voluminosi capelli neri. Fu allora che imparai a legarmi un fazzoletto in testa. Al suono delle campane che annunciavano mezzo giorno, la tumultuosa enorme trebbia smetteva di ronzare, tutti ci sedevamo per terra intorno ad una candida tovaglia sulla quale era sparso un sontuoso ed abbondante pranzo all'ombra di una quercia gigante i cui rami ci davano l'ombra e la protezione dal sol leone di luglio e c'invitava a fare un pisolino. Il mio piatto preferito era pipi e patatefritti alla perfezione con un sughettodentro il quale intingevamo il pane crostato preparato dalle piccole ma forti della mia zia ed infornato nel forno a legna.

Zia Albina possedeva molte proprietà che richiedevanomolti lavoratori, inclusi i suoi figli specialmente dal mio prezioso Luigi, un ragazzo intelligente con una memoria di ferro ed un'etica di lavoro che lo distingueva dagli altri membri della famiglia. Adoravo la mia zia ma ne risentivo dal fatto che dipendesse molto su Luigi. Ogni domenica andavo in chiesa con lei e le stavo accanto pregando che diventasse più generosa verso il mio caro Luigi dandogli l'opportunità di studiare. Mi piaceva sentirla cantare a squarcia gola esibendo una voce robusta e brillante diversa dalla mia, timida ed infantile. La mia Zia era una donna forte e piccola d'apparenza con un animo sensibile che si manifestava dalle numerose lacrime che le grondavano dai suoi piccoli occhi come la fontana vicino casa sua. Avevo una reverenza particolare per questa cara zia che sapeva dominare l'uomo e la natura.

RITA, MIA CUGINA

Rita, la più giovane delle figlie della zia Albina cresciuta dalla saggia zia Micuccia, sorella del Nonno Luigi, la quale adottò prima la zia Albina e poi le prese cura dei suoi numerosi figli mentre la loro mamma si dedicava totalmente all'agricoltura, il vero amore della sua vita. Io non conobbi molto la nostra Rita durante la sua crescita, ero emigrata in America, però nonostante l'oceano che ci separava ogni qual volta che ritornavo in Italia andavo a Vibo a trovarla, sposata con Mimmo un uomo di grande bontà e talenti dotato da una voce soave che rallegrava il creato. Il mio penultimo viaggio in Italia fu' un grande evento. Mimmo preparo' un memorabile cenone per noi tutti cugini e fu allora che Rita divenne mia figlia, scambiandoci storie intime della nostra esisteva. Fu allora che Rita mi diede la prima lezione di vita dove il perdono diventa atto di guarigione e dimenticanza. Fu allora che conobbi la sua adorata figlia Antonella, una psicologa infusa d'arte e di creatività' allucinante: lei dipinge, insegna usando teatro e teatrini con pupazzi particolari per provocare la conversazione e lo scambio di idee. I bambini l'adorano bensìi clienti adulti che vede nel pomeriggio ascoltando attentamente le loro storie di sofferenze senza pregiudizi dalla sua parte. Che famiglia d'artisti, chi dipinge, chi crea paste preziosissime, panettoni, torroni, gelati e torte. Rita crea con i bambini a scuola giochi, teatrini, e soprattutto li ama molto, un amore che fa sorridere queste creature con problemi fisici e mentali che solo l'amore e la comprensione può fare dimenticare anche se temporaneamente.

L'unico membro della famigliola che non ho incontrato durante questo viaggio fu Basilio il quale era in Francia ad eseguire gli studi d'ingegneria. Quando seppe al suo ritorno che io ero stata in Italia, anche se non conoscendomi, li avevamo visti due o tre volte quand'era ragazzino, decise di telefonarmi chiedendomi se poteva venire a trovarmi. Io gli risposi di venire quando voleva e nel frattempo di poche ore mi informa che aveva già comprato il biglietto e mi chiese per quanto tempo poteva rimanervi. Gli risposi quanto voleva solo che si sarebbe annoiato stare a lungo con due vecchi. Basilio arrivo' e rimase con noi per lungo tempo il che ci fece molto piacere; conobbe la mia Licia, son Giuliano e Jeremiah nonchè Murray, il papà di Jeremiah con il quale legò una stretta amicizia. Passavamo le mattinate in giardino insegnandogli l'Inglese, una lingua che voleva imparare a tutti i costi, ma a mezzogiorno era stanco dell'Inglese e mi chiedeva di parlare l'Italiano perché era intontito. Dopo pranzo il solito pisolino e poi andavamo a visitare questa bellissima città, Boston, con Giugliano facendogli da Cicerone e Licia conducendolo a Harvard che lei conosceva molto avendo insegnato là per cinque anni. Quanto ci siamo divertiti. Basilio voleva trovare lavoro quì a Boston e fece molte domande di lavoro ma non riuscendoci tornò in Italia dove eseguì un altro master in ingegneria a Roma sponsorizzato da un'impresa Italiana sita in America. Basilio fu ammesso e venne in America lavorando a Cleveland visitandoci quando il lavoro glielo permetteva.

Rita incominciò a venire in America a visitare Basilio e noi passando un pò di tempo quì a Boston. L'ultima volta Rita venne col fratello Luigi verso il quale nutre un profondo affetto. Ci siamo tanto divertiti passando delle belle giornate insieme che hanno approfondito la nostra vicinanza. Poi è arrivato il Covid che ha interrotto tutto, ma spero che una volta che l'epidemia passi possiamo rivedere la nostra Rita.

LA MIA MAMMA, DUE SETTIMANE PASSATE A TORONTO CON LEI

Sono le quindici e quaranta del quindici Febbraio del due mila e tre. Il treno entra in stazione con venti minuti d'anticipo. Ne sono lieta poiché ho il tempo d'ammirare ancora una volta, con più calma questa meravigliosa città che si chiama Toronto ed il perché non lo so. Mia madre sarà già alla finestra per vedermi scendere dal tassì, ma non me ne faccio una colpa se dileguo il mio passo... tanto le mamme sanno aspettare. Come è bello respirare l'aria fresca di questa mia città anche se il suo costante vento mi porta via il cappello, il quale libero anch'esso, se ne va a spasso per i fatti suoi fra il traffico assordante. Non gli corro dietro, è inutile cercare d'afferrarlo, sembra che anch'esso è in fretta, in fuga con la marea di gente che corre chi a destra, chi a sinistra, chi attraversa la strada senza tener conto delle macchine per raggiungere il Royal York, che se ne sta lì impalato di fronte la stazione, a guardare e fare i fatti propri. Questo monumento, immutabile al tempo, è tale e quale lo vidi quella prima sera del tredici Novembre, mille novecento cinquanta sette. Esso se ne stava piantato sul marciapiede come un colosso, muto ed impervio al mio dolore ed alla mia gioia—dolore costante dell'emigrante che abbandona la sua terra per un mondo ignoto, per un colosso che se ne sta muto; alla mia gioia di riabbracciare mio padre. La sua facciata luminosa sarà per me un punto di riferimento.

Anche io me ne sto là impalata come un lampione, a guardare quella folla sfuriata, un formicaio in corsa parlando, borbottando chi in Francese, Portoghese, Arabo, Inglese, Spagnolo... mi sentivo rinascere in un grande mondo armonioso, anche se un mondo in fretta. Quanto mi manca questa mia città; siamo cresciute insieme—essa, una metropoli, non più una cittadina di provincia; io, una donna, non più legata ad un villaggio tra monti e mare. Siamo entrambe uscite dall'infanzia del provincialismo degli anni cinquanta... quando una sera avvolta dalla notte e da un mantello di neve misi piede, valigetta di cartone in mano, e dopo un brutale viaggio in un battello sgangherato ed un treno a passo di lumaca. Che bufera di neve, che ventaccio penetrante nelle ossa anche dei più incappucciati. Persi il fiato per un attimo finchè un abbraccio caloroso mi colse a volo e vi rimasi in quelle braccia Ercolee finchè i miei occhi smisero di piovere sulla spalla di mio padre. Mi era tanto mancato il mio papà, separati dall'oceano per lunghi anni, ma la stazione ferroviaria di Toronto ci ha riuniti, e ci accolse nel suo buio e nel suo freddo... pellegrini smarriti nel suo suolo.

Il tassì si ferma davanti casa e mi lascia sul marciapiede con valige, valigette e cartella e riparte come un uragano. Forse aveva vergogna di essersi perso, di avermi condotta per strade e stradine, ignoto del mio grande desiderio di riscoprire la mia città non più avvolta nel velo infantile. Volevo ringraziarlo ed accoglierlo, benché rassicurarlo che anche io, emigrante mi perdo spesso nel mio vagar, e che il nostro Inglese, malgrado la nostra diligenza, riterrà in aeternum quel saporino di altre terre. Alla nostra città non importa nulla della nostra pronuncia, da dove veniamo o dove andiamo o se anche ci perdiamo nelle sue strade che le danno la vita. Da madre saggia e buona, essa ci accoglie nel suo grembo e ci integra nella sua tessitura facendone di ognuno di noi parte dell'insieme, parte integrale del suo splendido mosaico dove ogni mattonella, benchè diversa in colore e misura, è indispensabile nel creare l'insieme di diversità e nello stesso tempo di unità. Toronto è veramente d'ammirare, basti guardare e ci si ritrova nel piccolo della mattonella mosaica, perdendosi nell'immensità di questa sacra ed immensa terra che chiamiamo Canada.

La mia mamma è alla finestra, naso contro il vetro, mani in aria che gesticola facendomi segno di sbrigarmi. Poi scompare. Scende pian piano le scale una donnina dai capelli bianchi e grigi come la nebbia, occhietti sfondati nel viso rugoso dal tempo, un sorriso sfiora le sue labbra ed una mano tremante ma ancora forte. Con voce vigorosa e vibrante capace ancora di dare comandi e rimproveri dice: Che brutta bestia il tassista, se ne è andato di corsa come un dannato senza darti una mano con i bagagli... che canaglia. Toronto non è più la stessa città, è cambiata ora che ha aperte le sue porte a tutta questa razza di gente. Ma che diamine c'è in questa valigia! Che lumaca che sei, ti porti tutto dietro.

Valigia in mano, ancora intonando il suo miserere, saliamo le scale pian pianino nel buio. Io le sto dietro carica come un mulo, per rievocare una delle sue frequenti frasi al mio arrivo, e man mano che saliamo le ripide scale un profumino già a me noto invade le mie narici. Arrivati sul pianerottolo, giriamo a destra ed entriamo in un grande salotto con divano e poltrona d'epoca blu scuro entrambi coperti dalla plastica protettrice, incorruttibile dal tempo. Mi sembra che mia madre voglia fermare il tempo ed annientare la polvere... Mettiamo le valigie in un angolo della stanza su un panno bianchissimo di lino dicendomi: Chissà quanti micobri sulle valigie, hanno toccato molti pavimenti. Subito dopo andiamo in bagno a lavare le suole delle scarpe, anch'esse sudici come le valigie e messe nel corridoio su un altro panno bianco ad asciugarsi. "La città è sporca, non bisogna portare dentro quello che le sue strade ci offrono." Subito mi dà le pantofole da me usate negli ultimi trenta anni... pantofole che non hanno mai visto la luce del sole dal giorno in cui mia madre le comprò. Mi lavo le mani, il viso, e solo ora che mi sono pulita le posso dare un breve abbraccio, e le nostre guance si sfiorano appena. Niente eccessi, mia madre è una vera minimalista negli affetti.

Entriamo in cucina, un buco di stanza con minimi accessori, l'indispensabile; ma era una stanzetta dominata da un'enorme finestra attraverso la quale entrava un mare d'intensa luce. La tavola rettangolare contro il muro vicino alla finestra era ben apparecchiata con la solita tovaglia di lino da lei tessuta al telaio. Anche la tovaglia come la sua padroncina mostrava segni d'età, consunta dal tempo, ma ancora candida come la neve. Era la stessa tovaglia che assieme ad altre poche robe, miracolosamente sopravvisse quel micidiale viaggio transatlantico in un battello sgangherato. Niente in questa casa viene buttato via... tutto parla d'angosce, di gioie, d'interminabile lavoro, di vite vissute sotto un altro cielo, in un altro mondo mediterraneo dove le gioie e le angosce, come il sole e l'ombra si uniscono, si distaccano ma mai l'ontani gli uni dagli altri. Sì, questa tovaglia diventata una reliquia ancora usabile che vuole sfidare il tempo e preservare altri tempi e far si che non vengono sepolti dalla polvere che impercettibilmente ci circonda. Il sole brillava ancora su quella tovaglia di puro lino come brillava sulla testa bianca di mia madre dando entrambe un aspetto giovanile e rendendole felici di esser ancora utili.

La tovaglia di lino sfiorata ancora dal tramonto sembrava di sorridere, contenta di poter essere ancora di servizio nonostante i numerosi rammendi. Una vita lunga è stata la sua anche se l'orlo con il suo punto giorno reggeva a pena; un ricamo delicato che richiedeva molta luce per eseguirlo bene, oppure diceva mia madre la vista di un pilota. Ma quanto c'è voluto per creare questa benedetta tovaglia! Quanto c'è voluto che quel minuscolo seme diventasse tovaglia... Piantare quei semini, annaffiarli e nutrirli e poi quando erano diventati steli lunghi si raccoglievano e portate al fiume dove immersi nell'acqua diventavano morbidi per estrarre la fibra dal fusto... che massacro! Vedo ancora la mia mamma curva su una pietra gigantesca assidua a pestare con un macigno in mano quel fusto già macerato dalle acque del fiume. Quanta forza! Io da bambina ne soffrivo a vederla e nella mia testolina di bambina credevo di sentire quella pianta gridare: lasciatemi in pace, voglio tenere per me la mia fibra preziosa che è la mia vita. Il cuore mi batteva forte forte per quella povera pianta, il cui grido nessuno lo sentiva. L'ho vista crescere, quella pianticella in un campo circondata di fiori selvatici; accudita dalle stesse mani che ora la picchiavano. Le piante di lino ci hanno dato dei fiori celestini che noi bambini facevamo dei bei mazzolini per portarli alle maestre. Ma mia madre non pensava alle piante di lino, non aveva pietà, continuava il suo lavoro con serietà ed esibiva grande forza come se il demonio, uscito fuori dal mio libro di catechismo si fosse impadronito di lei, entrando nel suo animo e renderlo forte. Non mi piaceva più, la mia mamma. Io, presa dalla paura, mi rifugiavo dietro un enorme cespuglio di ginestra ai fiorellini gialli che emanavano un profumo incantevole che mi calmavano e mi facevano sognare di un mondo migliore. Questa vignetta ogni qual volta che emergeva dalla mia caverna di ricordi mi stringeva l'animo.

Alzo gli occhi da quella tovaglia e me la vedo, mia mamma, intenta a pestare col matterello le cotolette per renderle più soffici e sottili. Mi metto a ridere ma lei non se ne accorse intenta al suo lavoro. Le cotolette fritte erano pronte e ci sediamo a tavola ad un pranzetto delizioso e divoriamo tutto come due lupetti. Incominciamo con un brodetto di pollo con dentro pastina, seguito con le cotolette e molti contorni: pisell, peperoni arrostiti, melanzane ripiene, rapini affogati all'olio d'olivo, olive di ogni dimensione ed il pane da lei fatto con la crosta alla calabrese. Tutto un insieme di colori e sapori mediterranei.

POST SCRIPTUM

Un bel piatto di frutta fresca come dessert completa la nostra abbondante cena. Facciamo a gara chi arriva per primo a lavare i piatti, ma lei mi spinge dicendomi che tocca a lei pulire la cucina pochè io ero stanca dal viaggio. Mi arrendo e mi siedo al tavolo e la guardo con meraviglia ed ammirazione. I miei occhi si posano di nuovo su quella tovaglia e mi sembra di sentire quel ritmo costante del telaio dove mia madre scompariva ogni sera dopo cena. Io la seguivo come un cagnolino e me ne stavo seduta su unasediolina fatta dal nonno, e la guardavo come faccio ora. Il suo atelier era in uno stanzone con un enorme telaio; tutti quei fili, quelle corde, quei pettini sospesi in aria... mi sembrava di essere davanti ad un teatro di marionette, ognuna aveva la sua parte da recitare, i suoi fili da tirare. Mia madre era la direttrice, conosceva bene il suo mestiere. Con destrezza essa alzava con la mano sinistra la parte inferiore del telaio che rassomigliava ad un grande pettine per separare i fili, e poi vi infilava tra questi fili la navetta, un oggetto raffigurante un piccolo battello che trasportava i fili e velocemente senza esitare cambiava mano per afferrare la navigante navetta. Poi riassettava il nuovo filo facendo discendere il pettine e subito lo alzava con la mano sinistra e con la mano destra v'infilava la navetta, trasportatrice del filo... e la procedura si ripeteva per ore ed ore alla luce del lume ad olio. Io guardavo quella navetta navigare, quella bocca del telaio aprirsi e chiudersi con un ritmo instancabile. Immaginavo la bocca di un grande squalo che aveva lasciato il suo mondo d'acqua per conoscere il mondo del telaio, il mio mondo. Quante cose sapevano fare le mani della mia mamma, non stavano mai ferme sempre lavorando non avendo il tempo per accarezzare bambini o le figlie, o a stringersele al cuore che batte sempre più forte nel suo petto angosciato. Le sue angosce erano molte: le campane suonavano a martello, lei sempre pronta a dare una mano; a lavare e vestire la dolce fanciulla colta prematuramente dalla falce mietitrice di luglio. Vestita di bianco con le chiome nere come la notte cadenti su quel viso di cera, un mazzolino di fiori di campo raccolti da noi bambine nelle sue marmorie mani. Mia madre le dava l'ultimo tocco, un rosario di perline bianche intrecciato nelle dita. Mia madre era soddisfatta del suo lavoro, lo vedevo tutto nel suo triste viso dal buco della chiave mentre le vicine mi esortavano d'andare a casa altrimenti la Scarlattina avrebbe troncata anche me.

Io non avevo paura della Scarlattina, poiché la mia mamma non aveva paura, era là a vestire la bambina; ne ero orgogliosa della mia mamma mentre le vicine se ne stavano fuori impalate come sagome. Mia madre uscì dalla casa della morta e mio padre là che l'aspettava con un litro di alcol per disinfettarla e poi bruciare i suoi indumenti. La sera quando eravamo tutti radunati nella sala da pranzo, il nonno ci raccontava le storie dei cow boys nell'ovest dell'America. Mia madre ascoltava ma le sue mani non trovavano pace se non in movimento: filava la lana per fare le magliette calde al nonno il quale mentre era con i cow boys si prese una bella polmonite che lo lasciò sofferente in aeternum. Io mi facevo il calcolo nella mia testolina di bambina... come fa una polmonite durare dal mille ottocento novanta al mille novecento cinquanta... era polmonite di cow boys mi dicevo... forse è particolare poiché non avevo il coraggio di chiederlo al nonno. Le mani di mia madre andavano per conto proprio, avevano il loro ritmo, un ritmo perpetuo. Lei ascoltava ma non sentiva, era immersa nel mondo del domani: una lista di lavori l'attendeva al chiaro dell'alba: Ah le uova del baco da seta dovevano essere riscaldate lievemente per svegliarli dal loro sonno di uovo ed incominciare a brulicare; un lavoro delicato, troppo calore avrebbe distrutto le uova, poco calore avrebbe fermato la magica metamorfosi. Noi bambine eravamo già arrampicate sui gelsi per raccogliere le foglie che nutrivano i bachi e trasformarli in preziosi bozzoli bianchi. Il baco mangia tante di quelle foglie che una volta raggiunto un peso anormale, sazio a non poterne più, si mette a sputacchiare finchè non diventi uno bozzolo chiuso nel suo sepolcro. Io ne ero incantata da quel fenomeno e non volevo andare a letto e perdere quella trasformazione magica. La mia mamma era pronta ad andare al fiume a fare i bucato, una cesta di biancheria sudicia l'aspettava. Con forza Erculea metteva la cesta sulla testa e via verso il fiume. Ah! Quel fiume... io saltellavo nell'acqua, poi correvo dietro le farfalle, facevo una ghirlanda fi fiori e me la mettevo sulla mia testa, mentre mia madre china insaponava la biancheria col sapone da lei fatto. Poi metteva la biancheria nella cesta, un fazzoletto in forma di corona sulla testa per sostenere la cesta. Mia madre camminava diritta come una canna, sembrava una ballerina. Ogni tanto cambiava braccio per reggere la cesta mentre io saltellavo come un grillo dietro di lei.

Arrivate a casa, la biancheria veniva messa in un enorme vaso di terracotta con un buco alla parte inferiore a forma di pene sul quale vi versava l'acqua bollente con le ceneri del caminetto e lasciava il tutto scolare durante la notte per poi l'indomani portarla di nuovo al fiume per sciorinarla nelle acque limpide e stenderla al sole. Io mi divertivo a raccogliere la creta dalla terra e formare le figurine per il presepe. Una volta asciutti, mia madre mi dava dei colori da lei preparati per la seta ed io passavo ore a dipingerli.

Quante memorie, guardo la mia mamma e la vedo ancora china a lavare i piatti; com'è precisa, metodica e forte benché la sua avanzata età. Gli occhi piccoli e sorridenti ma stanchi, penetrano il mio animo che arde per il suo amore. Andiamo in salotto a guardare il televisore ed ascoltare il telegiornale in Italiano e ci spaventiamo: gli Americani incominciarono a bombardare Afghanistan, un'altra guerra. Mia madre chiude gli occhi per un attimo, e mi chiede scusa per la sua sonnolenza. "Sono vecchia! Che brutta bestia è la vecchiaia. Combattono ancora?" mi chiede ed il suo sguardo si allontana, chi sà cosa sta pensando e dove stà andando. Forse pensa alle guerre che lei ha vissute, puntando il suo pensiero su quel momento, indelebile nella sua mente quando seduta sulle ginocchia della sua mamma (5 anni) coglieva col suo dito le lacrime che cadevano dai suoi occhi neri e limpidi. Perché piangeva? Per quel colosso d'uomo col cappello a bersaglio dalle lunghe piume che li salutava forse per l'ultima volta. Diede un bacio alla mia mamma e le disse: Non ti vedrò mai più, ed il bersagliere partì per sempre a combattere al fronte della guerra del quindici–diciotto.

"Com'è brutta la guerra, ci ruba i nostri cari e ci strazia il cuore" e con queste parole la mia mamma apre gli occhi allo spettacolo orribile di gente che corre chi a destra, chi a sinistra verso qualche rifugio per proteggersi sia dale forze Talibani che dalle bombe Americane che cadevano come foglie dagli alberi battuti dall'uragano. Mia madre chiude di nuovo gli occhi per non vedere e nascondere le lacrime che scorrevano come l'acqua della nostra fontana in Capistrano. Si chiude in un silenzio di tomba; forse pensava agli anni quaranta quando lei come le donne Afgane correva verso Serra San Bruno, bambine in braccio, un'altra nel grembo, a trovare riparo. Dopo un lungo ed arduo viaggio, arrivati a Serra, si accamparono vicino al monastero, chiedendo protezione a San Bruno, il fondatore dell'abbazia. Anche San Bruno scappò via da Roma e trovò rifugio fra gli abeti giganteschi. Mio padre, con l'aiuto di alcuni amici costruì una capanna con un sotterraneo, rifugio durante i bombardamenti.

Spensi il televisore e le sedetti vicina sfiorandole amorosamente le guance; era così assorta nel suo pensiero che sembrava totalmente assente. Mi strinse la mano fissandomi negli occhi: "Ah! Le guerre! Che disastro che sono, rubano a chi la vita ed a coloro che la sopravvivono, la pace. Non ci sono vincitori nelle guerre, perdiamo tutti una parte di noi stessi... la voglia di continuare, tale è la devastazione e la disperazione. Ma io dovevo continuare, avevo te da crescere e spesso mi chiedevo perchè ti ho portata alla luce e perché... per soffrire come me. Cosa potevo offrirti, un mondo dove anche i buoni diventano cattivi a furia di soffrire. Ma nonostante la fame tu sei voluta nascere in questo mondo non mondo." La colpa era sempre mia per mia mamma: non solo avevo scelto la vita, ma nacqui femmina; è venuta in Canada per me dove si sente vittima... Mia madre non ne aveva voglia di parlare della mia nascita. Ogni qualvolta glielo chiedevo mi rispondeva di chiederlo alla mia zia Maria, la quale mi raccontò la triste storia due giorni prima della mia partenza. L'Oddissea Numero Uno (il mio libro) descrive il completo evento: nacqui sotto il ponte vicino al frantoio del nonno il quale tentò di zittirmi per sempre mettendo la sua mano gigantesca sulla mia bocca che gridava per la fame...

"La guerra non finisce mai" dice mia madre totalmente sveglia e m'invita d'andare in cucina e bere il tè nelle sue tazze preferite di porcellana inglese a fiori, festose, leggere e quasi trasparenti; il tè anch'esso leggero accompagnato da un taralluccio fatto da lei e che mangiava con tanto gusto come se fosse la prima volta. Mia madre sapeva cogliere il momento, la guerra era lontana dal suo pensiero, ora era il momento di celebrare il nostro essere insieme nella sua limpida cucina. Volevo abbracciare la mia vecchia e stringermela al cuore che batteva di gioia d'essere con lei e di rimorso per averla lasciata per un'altra terra. Non osai, aveva il raffreddore e mi avrebbe rimproverata. Quando ha il raffreddoreessa creded'avere la peste; ha paura del contagio benché si lavi le mani continuamente; non accetta carezze, e saluti da vicino. Anche la vecchiaia è per lei una malattia contagiosa, non permette che nessuno usi il suo pettine dicendo: "E un oggetto di vecchia, ti potrebbero cadere i capelli". L'asciugamano è un'altra reliquia della vecchiaia, intoccabilealle mani altrui. Anche il suo candido letto era vietato, non ci potevamo avvicinarci a darle un bacio prima che si addormentasse poiché non ha la dentiera e la sua bocca cavernosa rimaneva chiusa fino al mattino.

Mia madre ha una filosofia medica particolare specialmente per il diabete: una spremuta di limone abbassa lo zucchero dopo aver ingerito numerose cioccolateal liquore. L'indomani si misura lo zucchero e tutto è a posto. Per lei il limone è il rimedio, peccato che la medicina non l'abbia ancorascoperto, diceva sempre. Alle nove precise fa colazione, niente eccessi e la sua giornata incomincia. E sempre occupata come lo era da giovane: fa il bucato con tutta l'attenzione dovutagli come lo faceva da sempre, ora beandosi delle comodità moderne specialmente della candeggina che l'utilizzava abbondantemente sia per rendere la biancheria bianca, sia per disinfettarla. Cerco d'aiutarla a stendere la biancheriasu fili bianchissimi anch'essi vittime della candeggina, ma non me lo permette dicendo: "Questo è un lavoro che richiede attenzione e voi giovani siete abituati al dryer." Quando porta sù la biancheria bien piegata in una cesta bianca, sembra che il sole o il vento gliel'abbia stirata. Sale le scale con la cesta in testa, sembrauna gazzella, non fermavaa riposarsi oprendere il fiato. Io la seguivo come facevo da bambina quando ritornavamo verso il nostro paese, mentre noi bambine le saltellavamo davanti festose come le donzellette del poema "Sabato del Villaggio" di Giacomo Leopardi fermandoci quà e là a raccogliere le fragoline del bosco che vanivano infilate in un lungo filo d'erba. Delle volte ci fermavamo sotto un gelso per raccogliere le sue foglie unico cibo per i nostri bachi di seta che aspettavo famelici il nostro ritorno. "Nessuno ritorna al villaggio a mani vuote" diceva il nonno seduto sotto un cacio entrambi centenari che predicava al vento. I bachi mangiavano ad nauseam non riuscivamo a riempire i loro stomachini finchè un giorno il loro brulicare finì e i bachi si trasformarono in palle bianche (bozzoli) che una volta asciugati nel forno tiepido, mia madre estraeva gomitoli di filo morbido e color grano. Noi bambine guardavamo quel filo che veniva fuori come una sergente d'acqua, e pensavamo ai nostri poveri bachi che per la loro voracità di mangiare a non finire causarono la loro morte, oh c'era qualche altro mistero che dominava questa metamorfosi? Io mi logoravo nel mio pensiero, la mia testolina di bambina di cinque anni non riusciva a risolvere questo problema, basta, bisogna aspettare finchè io cresca, e ritornavo alla mia pazza gioia di saltellare come un grillo.

Guarda com'è bella la biancheria una volta stirata, e con grande soddisfazione la metteva nei cassetti che profumavano di lavanda. Forse nel stirare la biancheria, mia madre rimuoveva anche le pieghe nel suo pensiero, le sue idee diventavano più chiare, più limpide ed un senso di pace discendeva nel suo animo, si vedeva dal suo viso ora luminoso come le stelle. Sembrava la giovanetta di anni fà nonostante i suoi novanta anni. Io adoravo guardare quel volto di Madonna, fiero, un pò rugato ma fresco come se fosse stato scolpito sulle cime del monte Coppari; un viso che racconta la storia del suo lungo cammino entro due secoli di vita.

Mentre ero a Toronto notai sul calendario che dovevamo andare dal medico per la visita annuale, una visita che mia madre crede non necessaria ma dopo tante insistenze, sono stata capace di convincerla d'andare. Dopo tante polemiche usciamo da casa, lei perfetta nella sua camicetta di seta, scarpe lucidissime di pelle borsetta a mano, occhiali di sole grandi dominavano l suo piccolo viso. Le aveva tolti da un porta occhiali di velluto avvolti in un tovagliolo di seta... un'altra delle sue reliquie. Camminiamo sullala strada Montrose che ci porta a College Street, dove il mondo della mia mamma esisteva seguendo un ritmo tutto suo. Entriamo in banca dove ella depositava i suoi risparmi e pensioncina, tutto nascosto in un sacchetto di seta legato alla cintura sotto la maglietta finchè eravamo davanti la cassiera. Traversiamo College ed entriamo nella Grotta del Formaggio dove comprava la ricotta e le mozzarelle freschissime, il pane fresco e croccante era appena uscito dal forno mandava un profumo irresistibile; entriamo e ne compriamo due o tre filoni. Entriamo la macelleria dove il macellaio appena la vide corse subito a lavarsi le mani, e poi ritorna pronto a servirla. Com'è esigente la mia vecchia!

Finalmente arriviamo alla clinica dove la sala d'aspetto è piena; mia madre guarda intorno e vede che c'è un posto libero, toglie dalla borsetta un fazzoletto e vi copre la sedia e poi si siede. L'infermiera ci chiama ed entriamo nella sala dove il medico ci aspettava. Ci sediamo, lei su un altro fazzoletto steso sulla poltrona ed io accanto. Il medico le dà un caro saluto stringendole la mano e le chiede come sta. E pericoloso fare una tale domanda a mia mamma, la risposta non è affatto semplice: una litania di malanni, mal di testa, giramenti di testa, dolori a destra ed a sinistra... Povero medico, non sapeva da dove incominciare, ma da medico intelligente lascia che si svuoti e dopo una lunga pausa incomincia a visitarla. Finita la visita usciamo fuori e lei contenta camminava come una donzelletta. Entriamo al bar a prenderci un cappuccino ed un dolce occupando sempre il posto in fondo per non farsi vedere dalla gente che passava ed evitare il malocchio. Cariche come due muli barcolliamo verso casa e subito andiamo a riposarci. Ma non potendo dormire mi venne in mente la storia di Licia, mia figlia, che spesso accompagnava la mia mamma dai medici. Durante una di queste visite dallo specialista per il mal di testa, Licia racconta: Entrano in ufficio e mia madre felice di essere di fronte un medico bello, alto, proprio come li voleva lei.

Doctor—When do you have the headaches? Licia traduce, quando ti vengono i mal di testa, nonna?

Nonna—Beh, quando vogliono! Licia, whenever they want!

Doctor—Before or after dinner or in the morning, or evening? Licia, prima o dopo pranzo, la mattina o la sera?

Nonna—Dottore. gliel'ho già detto—quando vogliono. Licia, I have already told you, whenever they like.

Doctor—And now how do you feel, do you have a headache? E ora come ti senti, nonna, hai il mal di testa?

Nonna—Dottore, mi sento male allo stomaco, perdo il bilancio, vado da un lato all'altro... Mi sento come un ubriaco... Licia non aveva bisogno di tradurre, la nonna oscillava da destra a sinistra come un pendolo.

Nonna—Lei, dottore, sà come si sente un ubriaco? Do you know how a drunk feels?

Dottore—No, I don't know... No, non lo so...

Nonna—Allora dottore, mi sento come morire, si butta sulla sedia e chiude gli occhi. Do you know how one feels when one is about to die?

Dottore—No I don't. No, non lo so.

Nonna—Andiamo, Licia, non sa come uno si sente quando è ubriaco. Non sa come uno si sente quando stà per morire... Che cosa può fare per me questo dottore.

Apre la borsetta, tira fuori un biglietto di cento dollari e glielo butta sul tavolino ed esce fuori. Licia rossa dalla vergogna non trovò parole. Strinse le spalle e corse fuori a rintracciare la nonna che era già fuori a sventolare le mani per fermare un tassì. Con Nonna ogni uscita è un'avventura.

L'indomani ero sul treno pronta a rievocare e narrare le due settimane magiche con mia madre.

www.ingramcontent.com/pod-product-compliance
Lightning Source LLC
Chambersburg PA
CBHW030433010526
44118CB00011B/615